# Fearless Social Confidence

## Strategies to Conquer Insecurity, Eliminate Anxiety, and Handle Any Situation

### *How to Live Freely*

By Patrick King, Social Interaction Specialist at www.PatrickKingConsulting.com

# Table of Contents

## Foreword – Dr. Aziz Gazipura

This might be the most valuable book you read in your entire life. Now, before you roll your eyes and blow this off as hype, hear me out.

I believe social confidence is the most important skill for creating an extraordinary life. No matter what you want, whether it's more love, friendships, dates, an amazing relationship, career success, the respect and admiration of your peers, money, inner peace, happiness, or amazing health, guess what? It's going to involve other people.

You are not going to achieve great things, feel connected, or be happy without other people in your life. In fact, over your lifetime you are going to have thousands, or even millions, of interactions. And the better you get at social confidence, the better you will feel as you engage with others. The better they will feel around you. The more they will want to be around you, become your friend, hire you, date you, sleep with you, or marry you. The more they will respect, admire, and cherish you.

And best of all, the more confident you are, the more you can let all these goodies in. You stop blocking out the success and love, and start really feeling proud of yourself and worthy and lovable.

I can say all this with absolute certainty because I've lived in both worlds. I lived with depressingly low social confidence for many years. Insecurity, comparisons, inferiority, self-doubt, and harsh self-criticism made up much of my daily inner world. I was never enough, and certainly not as good as Sam, or Chris, or Travis, or many others I regularly compared myself too. Not good enough to date, to hire, or to love.

I've also lived in another world. Where I am handsome, strong, and magnetically attractive. In this world I receive praise, admiration, and love. I attract more and more opportunities, success, and wealth into my life. I have amazing people that I look up to as my friends, mentors, and the best one of all became my wife!

Do you want to know how I travelled from one world to the other? What was the bridge? It's what Patrick will teach you in this book. It's studying and mastering the skill of social confidence. Which, after studying this for thirteen years and working with thousands of people, is something I know that every single human on this planet can do, if they are willing to learn, grow, and take action step by step.

What I love about Patrick is just how good he is at mapping out those steps. This book, like many of his others, doesn't just give you great insight into how social confidence works.

He also teaches you exactly how to do it, step-by-step.

The first time I read one of Patrick's books, I thought to myself, "wow, this is really good. Uh oh, he's better than me!" Ah, the path to ever-increasing confidence. But I smiled at this comparison, and settled in to learn, to grow.

And that is exactly what you will do as you read this book. Patrick is a master teacher and he has a gift for creating new and powerful strategies that help you boost your confidence now. He then communicates these strategies in clear, engaging ways that are easy to remember and use when you need them most.

I am excited for you. If you read this book all the way through, and apply what you learn, your life will never be the same again. You will bridge from wherever you are now to an entirely new world with more love, abundance, and joy than you realize. And once you're there, you will never go back.

With Love,

Dr. Aziz Gazipura
The Center For Social Confidence
Portland, Oregon
August 20, 2016

## Introduction

There was a time in my life when I was deeply uncomfortable placing my order at McDonald's.

However, it wasn't because I had inner turmoil about the massive load of saturated fat I was about to put into my body.

It was because I had to *speak to someone* to do it.

I remember one particular instance at an Applebee's. The waitress had come around to my side of the table to take my order, but I wasn't quite ready so I tried to stall her by asking her what she recommended.

I could sense her getting extremely impatient, the rest of the table staring at me and wishing I hadn't come, and the cooks in the back covertly planning to spit in my food.

I started sweating all over and my ears became so hot I thought they were going to melt right off my head.

I knew it was likely that I had blown things out of proportion and that I was making assumptions that couldn't possibly be true. But the negative self-talk in my head was overpowering any sense of rationality and it held me hostage.

I felt rushed and latched onto the first menu item my eyes landed on. When the food came, I ate it as quickly as possible, left some money on the table and, to my friends' protests, made up an excuse about having to go home.

At no point did I truly think I was acting irrationally.

When I speak about social confidence or the lack thereof, I'm speaking as someone who's been in your shoes and knows how it feels. I know how crippling and fear-driven it is, and how it can prevent you from living your life the way you want to.

But I also know how small, incremental victories and the spike of adrenaline that accompanies each one are the key to overcoming social awkwardness and lack of confidence.

And when I say small victories, I mean small – like making eye contact for more than one second on one day, and inserting one line of small talk in a conversation with a cashier or barista another day.

Then, doing both things on the same day and adding in a carefully rehearsed story about my weekend.

Developing and building social confidence is definitely a process.

And it's a process that can make you feel as high as a

soaring eagle, or as low as an earthworm.

Developing fearless social confidence is essentially developing the ability to create the life you want and not shying away from social interaction and the opportunities that come with it.

It's the ability to live freely. Just hoping for the best does not work. Relationships are the most important facet of our lives, and viewing each one as a potential judgmental rejection is crippling and paralyzing.

How can you begin to soar?

## Chapter 1. The Ripple Effect of Social Confidence

There's a poetic saying that when a butterfly flaps its wings in Brazil, it causes a tsunami in Japan.

What does that mean?

It means that no matter how small an action, there will always be (sometimes far reaching) consequences from it that we probably will not realize at the time.

A butterfly might displace only a single breath's worth of air but as it travels that tiny flutter of air can easily snowball and aggregate into a monstrous tsunami. The aftereffects of our actions are often hidden, unintended, or flat-out ignored.

That's the ripple effect, and it operates in every situation with or without social confidence.

I want to start this book by taking a look at how your negative assumptions and your approach adversely affect you in your everyday life.

My clients often proclaim that when they finally achieve a level of social confidence (or fill in the blank measure of accomplishment), they'll be ready to take on the world, as if all along they were just missing that one catalyzing ingredient.

It's a great start, but unfortunately, only one of a multitude of steps. Why? The ripple effect.

The first step to social confidence is to realize how it affects your entire outlook on life, not just when you're at a networking event or a birthday party. Not feeling like you can speak freely out of a fear of judgment and rejection is more than just missing out on parties.

You might think that although low social confidence is the source of some discomfort – or that strong confidence brings some advantages – in the big scheme of things, it's not that big of a deal. You need to take a long hard look at just how your level of social confidence takes its toll.

The best way to understand the impact of low social confidence is to contrast people with high self-esteem and social confidence in social situations with people who have low social confidence.

People that possess high self-esteem and social confidence take almost all of the following for granted, and why wouldn't they? Shouldn't you?

**Socially confident people expect to be accepted.**

When they meet strangers, they *expect* to make a good impression and don't get entangled in or stymied by fears that they will be negatively perceived by others. They take for granted that people will react positively to them. They never approach situations thinking, "What if they don't like me?" Instead they think, "I hope I like them."

They have the same adrenaline coursing through their veins when they meet strangers, but it manifests as excitement, where for others it will manifest as anxiety.

**Socially confident people evaluate themselves positively.**

This is partially due to their healthy self-talk, and partially due to their positive self-perception. What does this mean?

They rate their social abilities through a positive baseline. If they do well, that's par for the course. They expected that. If they do poorly, it's an occasional exception that they can learn from. They don't allow themselves to be affected by singular incidents that they know don't represent their abilities. They have a positive self-image.

**Socially confident people can deal with criticism.**

Criticism doesn't crumble them. This is related to the previous point. Confident people learn to compartmentalize and separate criticism and recognize its actual purpose; they do not take it personally in an emotional way.

Their identity doesn't ebb and flow because of a single errant comment. It doesn't cause them to question their entire being or worth. They know they have worth even if they have faltered in a single area.

In fact, they seek criticism because they know they need it to improve and they will be better off for it. They are not afraid that criticism will confirm a harsh truth about themselves that they've been trying to avoid.

**Socially confident people feel comfortable around superiors.**

Define superior however you want – someone who is better looking, more athletic, higher in the office hierarchy, or more outgoing and charming. Socially confident people feel comfortable because they don't feel threatened, or that their flaws and vulnerabilities will be highlighted by the other person's qualities.

They can celebrate the talents and triumphs of others because they know that others' accomplishments do not diminish (and should not discourage) their own. They know the world doesn't run on an invisible currency that requires others to lose in order for them to win.

In fact, they look forward to spending time with "superiors" because they know that's the key to learning and bettering themselves, as opposed to revealing flaws.

Are these simple aspects of interacting with others a given in your mind?

In contrast, how do people who lack social confidence approach social situations?

**People without social confidence expect rejection.**

Before they even step into a social situation, in the back of their minds they are already anticipating failure. They're looking for cues that people are disinterested or bored with them. They think twice before speaking and effectively (and prematurely) censor themselves.

They are already thinking they will make fools of themselves so they expect the worst-case scenario. This shows in their facial expressions and body language, and does indeed cause people to react poorly to them. They cause their worst-case scenario to come true because they never allow themselves to be vulnerable or open up to others.

When you expect rejection, you feel helpless, as if nothing you can possibly do will make a difference. Following that logic, why would you leave your home to try at all?

**People without social confidence evaluate themselves negatively.**

In stark contrast to the socially confident version, unconfident people evaluate themselves from a baseline of negativity. If they perform well, they view it as an isolated anomaly. They shock themselves.

They expect the worst from themselves and thus often get it because they have set themselves up to fail. Their preconceptions have, in their minds, made it okay for them to perform poorly.

When you set your expectations low, you skirt disappointment. That might provide a small level of comfort to you, but it means you will not strive to improve and therefore never give yourself the chance to realize how much better life can be.

In fact, higher standards scare low confidence people. They're not sure if they will be able to cope.

Part of this is admittedly a defense mechanism aimed at lowering expectations to stave off rejection.

**People without social confidence despise criticism.**

Criticism is a nightmare for the unconfident.

On the surface they might want to put up a fight, but deep down they feel the criticism is warranted and deserved. They can't defend themselves with conviction because they don't believe in themselves.

Their self-perception already hangs on a thin thread, so any small criticism can sever that thread and plunge them into a dark abyss of negativity. It's a crack in their armor that is representative of their entire value as a human being.

Worse, they feel whatever shortcoming they've been attempting to conceal will be exposed by criticism. And then they will have to face the harsh reality of their shortcomings.

Unconfident people will steer clear of the spotlight and taking action as a way of avoiding negative feedback that will confirm their worst fears.

**People without social confidence are highly uncomfortable around superiors.**

Unconfident people are threatened by those they view as superiors.

This is fueled in equal parts by jealousy, lack of confidence, and viewing social situations as zero sum games – there can only be one winner, so everyone else has to be a loser (including them).

Unconfident people feel they *have* to lose out in social situations. The worst part about this viewpoint is that they are more than happy to assume the role of loser.

They feel swept up in a tornado when someone who is socially superior comes by. They feel discouraged and dejected because they see someone who represents something they can never be. Furthermore, they compare themselves to their superiors in a way that emphasizes all their own shortcomings.

See what I mean by the ripple effect?

What appears to be one relatively small shortcoming (lacking social confidence) ultimately permeates how the social unconfident person approaches every person they encounter in their daily life.

This level of social fear is truly preventing you from living your life to the fullest potential, because what is life if not relationships?

You encounter people in the office, in your neighborhood, and even when you shop for groceries or get a cup of coffee. What assumptions do you hold about your social confidence? And where along the spectrum do you fall when you think of yourself walking into those situations?

You lack of confidence might mean you fail to meet that new person who can open new doors of opportunity as far as your career and social life go. You may even have met somebody that you're extremely interested in, but you let your fears get the better of you.

Whatever the case, you were held back in a way that has become so second nature that you no longer think of looking at certain social situations as opportunities.

Instead, you draw a line in the sand as to where you can go, how far you can go, and what is worth your effort. As time goes on, this self-created circle of social capability, competency, and confidence begins to collapse and shrink. Eventually, you'll feel trapped.

If you stay where you are, you're standing in a sealed room that is quickly filling to the top with water.

You cannot stay where you are. You cannot continue to keep running away from your social anxiety and fears. You need to act. If you don't change, nothing will happen.

Low social confidence can cripple you.

You will have imprisoned yourself behind invisible bars. You can do whatever you want, but you choose not to because of these invisible walls – walls that were *not* created by people who have it out for you. There are no evil ogres keeping you down. Just you.

Social confidence can make you feel like the king of the world. Ultimately, it's your choice.

You are very familiar with the patterns. You feel anxious around other people. This anxiety and the accompanying discomfort makes you engage in anti-social behavior. As a result, you receive negative or lukewarm feedback. You internalize this feedback and create an even more meek and uncomfortable version of yourself. Anxiety builds and you sink deeper into social quicksand.

Do you want to climb out of the quicksand?

## Chapter 2. Banish Your Negative Self-Talk

When I was younger, I vividly recall making a presentation on owls.

It went poorly, to say the least. I fumbled over my opening sentence, tripped on the easel that was holding up my poster, and for the grand finale, I committed a Freudian slip and said that owls hunted vermin and rodents such as my teacher.

I sat down in a puddle of sweat to sparse and confused applause. The first thing I did was start berating myself for every little thing that had gone wrong.

*How could I trip? I'm so clumsy!*

*How could I mess up the beginning! I'm so bad at speaking!*

*How could I call Mrs. Robinson a vermin? I'm so stupid!*

The talk itself probably wasn't as bad as I remember it; after all, I received an A- for it. It was one of my better speech grades in the class, actually.

But my negative self-talk, based on self-created assumptions, scarred me and scared me away from giving speeches for years after. The experience made me frame myself as "terrible at public speaking."

In one fell swoop, I had handily disarmed and minimized myself. Not only that, I had extended the impact of one isolated incident to a degradation of my character as a whole. Because I hadn't performed optimally on this one speech, I was now an objectively worse person than I was the day before I'd given the speech. I couldn't see the forest for the trees.

How could that be true?

That's the power of negative self-talk.

We use negative self-talk to explain situations that we can't assess objectively. When we react emotionally, we feel helpless to control our fates and practically refuse to see the light side of any situation.

The first step to making progress in addressing a lack of social confidence is to pay attention to how we talk to ourselves. Everybody has an internal monologue that plays on repeat. Everybody is always making quick mental judgments of the things playing out around them or the things they are observing.

We're not always aware of it and it runs subconsciously,

and that's what makes it so potentially dangerous. You never know how you end up with these thoughts until it's too late. That's how I ended up with a fear of public speaking for years afterwards – I didn't realize it stemmed from this formative experience and the associated negative self-talk.

If you have low social confidence, it's because you unknowingly use negative self-talk to make judgments and assumptions about yourself and others. You do this constantly and the judgments are flat out inaccurate.

You end up creating a narrative that is both damaging and disempowering. You feel socially weaker the more you engage in this self-talk. The worst part is you feel you can't stop, even if you can logically realize that it's not reality. All it takes is one little thing to push you over the edge.

What's worse is that it's incredibly common to suffer from the spotlight effect – that is, when you feel that everyone in the room is watching you and focusing on your every mistake. It compounds the dread.

You can't control your feelings and you feel this is completely natural and there is no other alternative reading to the things you observe.

What's more, you have the tendency to extend a judgment on a small aspect of your life to your entire being and existence. "I'm terrible at speaking" suddenly becomes "I can't deal with people at all."

**Negative Self-talk Patterns**

When you say to yourself that you aren't good enough or there's no reason why people should choose you, you are engaging in negative self-talk.

It's important that you pinpoint and clearly identify negative self-talk and know how to tell it apart from neutral or even positive self-talk. It's important to get ahold of negative self-talk because it leads to a slippery slope and huge downward spiral.

As the old saying goes, "If you repeat something long enough, eventually, you might believe that it's true." Of course, a lie even repeated a billion times, is still a lie. But it doesn't really matter if you believe it.

Your *perception* becomes reality when you keep repeating negative self-talk. The more you repeat it, the greater this downward spiral of negative mental states and negative external social responses will be.

Think of your stream of consciousness as a Facebook timeline.

There are all sorts of things that appear on your timeline. If you just let your negative mental habits filter everything, it's easy to think that all the items on your newsfeed or timeline are coming from a negative light. They just reinforce what you inaccurately already concluded about who you are, what you're capable of, and what your limits are in social situations.

These are all judgments and assumptions you've chosen to

create your reality.

You are subscribing to them and co-signing them. If you understand this, then you can take the opposite action, which is to edit what you choose to conclude. You can look at what you have been saying all along and contradict it or redirect it.

To make progress on this part, you have to understand the narrative you tell yourself.

Ask yourself: do you believe there's something wrong with you? Or that you're not good enough because of X, Y, or Z? Do you think you're not good enough because you don't have A, B, or C? And what do these believes say about your overall character?

This is not real.

These thoughts are arbitrary because everyone is different. People who have the same things as you, who come from similar backgrounds and who share similar experiences might actually have completely different self-talk. There are at least two primary ways to look at any situation, and there are limitless alternate explanations other than you being incredibly inadequate in something.

**Destroying Negative Self-talk through Self-analysis**

When you think you can't do something, or you feel you're making an excuse for something, the most important step you need to take is to *ask yourself why*.

The same applies to when you fail to attempt something out of fear of failure or rejection. Why did you feel the need to say that? Why is there a causal link between what transpired and how you feel?

Where does it come from? Who are you hoping to make feel better? What are the alternate explanations that don't involve you being inadequate, and what does this mean about your self-perception? And is there actual evidence or is it just an assumption based on emotion?

It's likely this isn't the first time you've resorted to negative self-talk to explain a situation.

Are there distinct facts or experiences from your personal history that created the assumptions you are now laboring under? What happened in the past for you to be conditioned to react this way? Are you letting a ghost from your past make you feel powerless and crippled yet still?

While it's okay to feel that you have a negative past or a negative experience, you need to make sure that negative perception is at least based on solid facts. What are the roots of your shame, regret, or fear?

For example, after a failed speech, you might be tempted to label yourself as a poor speaker in general.

That requires two causal leaps – (1) that you are a poor speaker, and (2) that the speech overall went poorly. What is your basis for believing these two things?

Are they objectively true, or is it just your subjective

assessment, based in negative emotions from the one phrase you stumbled over? Often, we assess our abilities as subpar based on a negative emotion attributed to one particular folly that no one besides ourselves cared about or even noticed.

Now look into the past.

Now that you can more accurately assess them – away from the influence of your emotions – how would you say your past speaking experiences have gone? Is there actually evidence and a track record to support your assumption that you are a terrible speaker? Or is there another, deeper reason for your feelings of fear and shame?

**Focus on Statements in the Moment**

When you make a statement to yourself like *I'm a loser, nobody likes me*, or *I'm not worth talking to*, pause and give yourself time and space.

Do the next four things in sequence.

First, ask yourself why you feel that way. What is the exact moment and action that caused the feeling? Is it something big, or small and isolated?

Second, what evidence is there to support that statement? Find the distortions and think about how a bystander might see the situation.

Third, think about alternate explanations for what triggered you to make that statement about yourself. Is the negative self-talk conclusion you're jumping to really what is happening? Life tends to unfold in a much simpler way than the conspiracies that tend to get cooked up in your head.

Finally, actively think about how you can rephrase your statement about yourself the way a person with high social confidence would.

A great analogy to this is when a friend or acquaintance takes a long time to respond to a text message.

You might assume they're angry with you, or annoyed that you wrote your text in a certain way. You might even think back through the past few weeks and come up with seven separate reasons for their being mad at you.

But if you give it enough time, go through this process, and you ask yourself certain questions, you will get a clearer picture. It's only been one hour, and they're in class or at work.

You're less likely to freak out if you think these things through. You'll end up dealing with the situation the way it should be dealt with; realistically and reasonably. And you'll be happier with your conclusions.

The bottom line is simple. Dealing with negative self-talk in an unhealthy way leads to a lasting lack of confidence and self-esteem. You're just digging yourself deeper and deeper into an emotional hole. You have to arrest this process. You have to make a decision to recognize that this is not you. This is not what defines you. This is not what you're all about or capable of.

One extremely effective way to deal with inner criticism and negative self-talk is to assign a name to the "speaker" of those statements.

Bob or Beth is the negative naysayer that lives in your brain. They know nothing and are always trying to tear you down, sometimes in ridiculous ways!

*"Oh, I'm being **soo** Bob right now. What about [insert your name here]? Where did he go?"*

Obviously, the speaker is you, but by intellectually and emotionally disassociating yourself from this negative stream of thoughts, you can create enough logical and intellectual distance to pick apart the criticism. It no longer becomes part of who you are so you can make progress and move beyond it. Also, this paves the way for you to more easily pick apart the internal criticisms because they are coming from someone else (Bob or Beth) and not from you.

# Chapter 3. Your Social Confidence Self-Assessment

One of the most underrated aspects of self-improvement is initial self-assessment.

If you wanted to set a goal to improve your one-mile run time, you first have to run a mile *without* training and record your time.

Not only your time, but how tired you felt, whether you had muscular or lung fatigue, when you starting feeling tired, and how you felt afterward. That's your self-assessment; your baseline.

This tells you exactly what you need to work on to improve, and what shortcomings you have that you might not realize. You might assume one thing about yourself, but the cold self-assessment won't lie to you and will reveal everything you need to know.

Suppose you wanted to improve your mile time, but you assumed all you had to do was work on your lung capacity because you do leg press exercises three times a week. You don't think muscular fatigue will be an issue. But what if by the first half mile, both your quadriceps are cramped? Your assumption was wrong even though it seemed to make sense when you made it.

The biggest value: you are able to see the difference between your *perceived* self and your *real* self.

In the same way, it's extremely important to conduct a self-assessment of your levels of social confidence to see exactly what situations and contexts drain you.

For you to make progress toward your desired destination, you have to have a clear idea of where you are now. It's really important to get a very clear survey of what you're dealing with.

Stop guessing at everything and try to hang your hat on something more solid. It is human nature to work only on the low hanging fruit and what's easy, and to stay away from real challenges. But being honest and challenging yourself is crucial if you want to truly make progress in your efforts to increase your social confidence.

Self-assessment enables you to find the truth and the difference between your real self and what you perceive yourself to be, and in regards to social situations, that's the difference in assuming that people hate you when in reality they like you.

By going through this process, you may realize that you are actually better or worse off than you imagined. What's important is that you go through it honestly and don't justify the answers you give. Your deeply rooted defense mechanisms may kick in.

If you consistently fall back on excuses, justifications, wishful thinking, or your worst fears, then no progress is possible. You're just wrestling with invisible alligators.

**Self-Assessment Questions**

The following are questions for you to honestly answer to get a clear idea of your social confidence – where it lies and where it does not.

Many of us feel "in the zone" when we feel confident about what we're talking about, or when there is structure. For others, structure and expectation puts immense pressure on us that makes us queasy to our cores.

Answering the following questions with a simple yes or no will tell you a good deal about what social confidence means to you, and what some of the possible causes are.

Make sure to think about all the circumstances involved in the following situations and articulate what about them makes you feel uneasy and uncomfortable.

Question 1

General Setting: Are you likely to ask for help in a store?

Question 2

Work Setting: Are you likely to volunteer to speak at a meeting?

Question 3

Social Setting: Are you likely to talk to a stranger at a friend's party?

Question 4

General Setting: Are you willing to complain about a wrong order in a restaurant?

Question 5

Work Setting: Are you likely to volunteer to lead a meeting?

Question 6

Social Setting: Are you likely to engage in small talk with a barista or cashier?

Question 7

General Setting: Are you likely to take the initiative and compliment someone?

Question 8

Work Setting: Can you handle confrontation and conflict?

Question 9

Social Setting: Are you likely to mean it when you ask people how they are?

Question 10

General Setting: Are you likely to welcome an opportunity to speak in public?

Question 11

Work Setting: Do you avoid hiding in your office all day and instead get out and interact with your co-workers?

Question 12

Social Setting: Are you likely to seek out old friends every weekend?

Don't think about these questions in terms of what you'd do on your best day, or think, "Yeah... I *could* do that."

Answer as you normally would the majority of your days and stop thinking about the ideal social self that you have pictured for yourself. Focus on how you actually behave. Focus on how you carry yourself in these very specific situations.

If you're having a tough time, just think back to the last time you found yourself in such a situation and focus on what you actually did.

We're trying to get an accurate picture of your social confidence level, not engage in wishful thinking.

After going through the above questions, ask yourself about the situations in which you *did* take social initiative and felt or exhibited social confidence. The key here is to pinpoint the kinds of circumstances in which you lack confidence and identify those areas where you're strong.

The three categories are significant because they indicate how and when you feel confident, and when you do not, depending on a range of factors.

If you are confident in a work setting but not the others, it means that you feel confident in your objective abilities. You are secure in your skills in this context and also feel confident and comfortable when you have a purpose you can hide behind.

When you have a role within a hierarchy that you can play, and you have strict boundaries, you feel fine if you stay within those boundaries. You can play a role just fine, as long as you aren't required to make too many independent decisions and have accountability rest on your shoulders.

You might feel incredibly insecure and clueless when you leave that safety, however. Without a clear purpose or role, how do you engage with others in a meaningful way? That's the reason many people hate the concept of "useless" small talk.

If you are confident in a social setting but not in others, it means you feel confident with people you already know well or when there is no real purpose and nothing at stake. You can socialize just to kill time, but the moment there is any pressure or expectation on you, you shrivel under the spotlight. If there is no expectation or even structure, you can do just fine with social confidence.

Presumably, these situations feel safe because you can leave them the moment you feel threatened.

You feel comfortable because nothing is expected of you and you can engage as little or as much as you like. You're not committing to anything, and you have freedom to keep yourself in a comfort zone of safety.

Most people have a mixture of the two categories. Keep in mind that these different situations might mean different things to different people. Whatever the meaning, you're discovering specifics as to your social confidence.

At this point, you should have two distinct images in your mind. On the one hand, you have a clear idea of who you *think* you are in social settings. This is based on your own perception.

On the other hand, you should also have a *clearer* idea of how you actually behave. The real world does not distinguish between our perceived selves and our real selves. It could not care less about our intentions, our motivations, or our other internal imaginings. All that matters is how we actually behave.

This exercise isn't meant to point out your shortcomings and make you depressed about them. Instead, it should empower you now that you have a clear mechanism for contrasting your perceived self (including its strengths and weaknesses) with your real self.

Now you're in a place to get ready to work.

## Chapter 4. Apples to Bananas Comparisons

One of my father's greatest flaws – and one he admits to – is his tendency to compare his achievements to those of his neighbors.

It's a classic case of feeling as if he has to keep up with the Joneses (or in his case, the Patels).

I never actually saw him do this, but when I was a kid, I swear he kept a list of every new contraption our neighbors bought. I remember him obsessing over their new car, which he pronounced "flashy and impractical," and yet gazed at longingly whenever we were outside.

It was as if there was nothing wrong with his life, so he had to manufacture things to agonize over and complain about.

He proved to me at a very young age that a surefire way to feel instantly lousy about your own life (and self) is to compare yourself with others.

Regardless of whatever strengths and qualities you bring to the table, you will become miserable when you compare yourself to others.

Even Bill Gates, one of the world's richest men, might feel lousy if he compares himself to certain people. If he compared himself to Michael Jordan in terms of basketball playing ability, Bill would come up severely short, pun intended.

By the same token, if Michael Jordan compared himself to Steve Jobs in terms of creativity and business acumen he might feel pretty inadequate as well.

But why should they?

They shouldn't feel bad because they have their own strengths and there's no reason for a basketball player to expect a high level of technological creativity, and vice versa. Yet they would. Comparisons are toxic, and worse, unnecessary – especially when you are comparing apples to bananas, which is almost always the case.

These kinds of comparisons might just be the number one thing that induces a lack of social confidence.

We have a tendency to compare ourselves to other people around us or to some kind of imagined ideal – neither of these situations is good.

For example, if you see that someone can do "X" and you can't do "X," it makes you feel inadequate and worthless.

*Amy can light up any room she enters. I could never do that.*

*Bob just went over and talked to that girl he didn't know. I could never do that.*

*Jim stood up in front of that crowd and gave an amazing speech. I could never do that.*

Well… who said you can't? And even if you're right, why would you judge your self-worth on a single trait or ability that doesn't particularly matter to you? The good news is it doesn't have to be this way.

Comparing is a learned habit that destroys your confidence because it tries to put all your value and worth into one tiny aspect. You have to understand that you are a compilation of many different traits and talents. You have your looks, your earning ability, your ability to play sports, how fast you type, and so on. These all matter.

In what way can only *you* connect with others? What are particular strengths you possess that can come in handy in social situations? What topics can you have a better conversation about than anyone? What about that one time you lit up the room and stole the show?

Unfortunately, when we compare ourselves to others, we ignore or throw out all the things we are good at and only focus on the one thing we're not good at or that we imagine others excel at.

The problem with comparing in a social setting is that we often carry with us a fictionalized ideal of how a "perfect" person would get along in particular social situations.

This person is about as real as Superman.

Unfortunately, we treat that notion as if it's absolutely real and we allow ourselves to feel crappy and inferior when we don't measure up. When we compare ourselves to this imagined ideal, we fail to see our strengths, value, and worth. If you keep doing this enough, your own social confidence will take a permanent beating.

You will start off in any kind of social interaction with an automatic deficit. And this built-in inferiority complex compounds over time.

Even if you come across someone who seems to have all the social graces and skills that match that idealized picture you have in your mind of a very adept social person, you're only looking at appearances. You may not be looking at who that person really is. Maybe that person is just a great actor.

When you compare, you only see what's on the outside, what people allow others to see about them. But what you're seeing isn't the whole picture and is not necessarily who they really are – it's just their very best version of themselves; the one they are willing to present to the world. You end up degrading yourself by choosing your darkest and worst view of yourself in comparison.

I repeat: you compare your *worst* moments to other people's *best* moments.

What if that public speaker nearly threw up before he

delivered the speech that you were so impressed by?

If we were more strategic (and realistic), we would recognize that everyone has a dark, less adept, less than perfect side. Remembering that will help you put them in a more realistic light. When you come across somebody who seems to have their act together, always keep in the back of your mind that this person is not perfect.

This person also has issues and insecurities like everyone else – like you. By always coming back to this central truth, you can throw some cold water on your natural tendency to elevate them and push yourself down.

The bottom line with comparisons is actually pretty straightforward.

Other people aren't only what they are showing to the world. Most people put on a good show. You probably know a couple that appears to get along great and be very much in love. They seem totally happy and to truly connect with each other in an enviable way. But do you really know what might be going on in their private life? Maybe they're on the brink of a divorce.

Take comfort from the fact that while there will be many people who are better at certain things than you are, there are also most certainly things that you will be better at. Keeping this in mind will enable you to have a more realistic set of expectations about yourself and others.

How can you use comparison to your social advantage?

**Think about why your friends like you.**

Think back to why you became friends with a certain person. It wasn't because you are the most social person in the world.

Whatever the currency, they found value in you and simply enjoyed your company. Focus on these values. Those can be foundations of increased self-confidence. You have to allow yourself to feel special because these people obviously found value in you. They could've been friends with others, but they chose you.

Figure out the talent that you bring to the table. Maybe it's your sense of humor. Maybe it's how comfortable you make people feel. Realize that this is what your friends come back to again and again. Allow yourself to feel good about the fact that you possess that trait and that maybe others don't.

Take your best friend. Now imagine a coworker. Why wouldn't they get along? Because you coworker isn't you! Now take this to a different level, and imagine that you invite friends from all different walks of life to a party together. Think about how you act differently with each group, and what makes you click with different people.

Why does each group like you? What special, unique presence to you bring?

The next time you beat yourself up with comparisons remember that they reflect the low opinion you have of yourself. They only exist because of your negative self-talk.

I mentioned in Chapter 2 how corrosive self-talk and your own negative personal narratives can be as far as your sense of self-worth and self-esteem go. Comparisons just add fuel to the fire.

If you ever need a mental reminder of how to deal with comparison, always imagine your favorite popular superstar sick with the flu, helpless on their bed. The people you look up to are still human beings and, being human, they have vulnerabilities. They may perform well in one particular aspect, but don't let that take away from the reality that they are just as human as you are.

**The next time you feel the compulsion to compare...**

Ask yourself these three questions.

First, do I have all the information about this person?

I'm going to guarantee the answer is absolutely no.

Madonna might be an awesome performer and Taylor Swift may have a great stage presence, but that's just one aspect of the different traits that make them up as a human being. How can you possibly assume that one particular person is perfect when you don't have all the information about that person? Maybe that person you truly admire beats up their kids or is mean to their parents. Maybe that person has issues with substance abuse.

The answer is always the same. You don't have all the information about the other person, so why would you put them up on pedestal? It's okay to put people up on a pedestal in terms of admiration, but never let that process result in your self-esteem taking a beating.

Second, are you judging yourself fairly?

Are you making a false comparison between someone's best and your worst, and letting emotion cloud your view of the situation?

Are you using someone's success to make you feel like a failure, or is someone's success only so because of your failure?

Third, is this trait that you admire and are focused on really something that defines your own value as a person?

Are you falling into the trap of thinking that a particular trait or set of traits you're comparing to your own is what defines you as a person, and what you should draw your self-worth from?

Don't do that.

For example, take Bill Gates. It's one thing to admire Bill Gates and his ability to spot an opportunity, create a winning company, and scale that vision up to benefit the lives of countless people all over the planet; it's another to look at Bill Gates's ability to make money as the crowning human trait that defines you as a person.

Is money what defines him as a person or what he draws his self-worth from?

Probably not.

## Chapter 5. Incremental Skill Cultivation

Confidence, if you truly think about it, is just the knowledge that no matter what happens, you can handle what is thrown at you.

If you're a confident musician, you'll feel comfortable performing a piece that you haven't played much before because you know you'll be able to figure it out or wing it. You can fill in the blanks and work off the other musicians.

If you're a confident soccer player, you'll feel comfortable playing pickup soccer and integrating into any team, knowing that you can be a plus on the pitch. You'll adapt just fine to any style of play.

And if you're socially confident? Well, you'll feel comfortable when you're thrown into any situation involving any group of people.

Social confidence is not an exercise in having all the answers all the time. Instead, as you can see, social confidence is about being *flexible and versatile*.

The key to the confidence of a soccer player or a musician is that they have smaller skills they feel they can depend on in times of stress or need – this is what makes them flexible and versatile. They don't have all the answers, but they can contribute in at least one meaningful way.

The soccer player thinks "I'm a great passer so I'll fit on any team" and the musician thinks "I'm a great sight reader so I can pick this up quickly."

These are small skills in the general scheme of their fields that they have successfully cultivated as sources of confidence. They've experienced the range of what can happen and know they can handle it. They allow this confidence to translate to other parts of their talents as a whole.

Of course, this is the same with social confidence. But if you can't think of one smaller social skill or talent that you can rely on and always come back to, it's going to be difficult to take a leap anywhere without any type of foundation or fallback.

Instead of aiming for some sort of grand theory of social interaction success, look to pick up small skills that you can then tweak to serve you well in a variety of social situations. When you cultivate your small skills, they will incrementally carry you toward greater success.

For example, if you knew that you had bulletproof stories or topics or jokes that you could always steer a social interaction toward, wouldn't you approach them more confidently? It dramatically expands what you feel that you can face, regardless of the context.

The lesson of this chapter is that confidence comes from knowing that you can do things. The more you can do without worry, the more confident you will become.

Start here and build bigger!

**Have a Calling Card**

Where the soccer player's calling card might be great passing, you have to explore and develop a *social calling card*.

This is something that you can always lean on and always know you're great at. It's your ace in the hole, your trump card, and occasionally your last resort.

If you're down in a conversation, or struggling to throw yourself into one, you can always resort to this calling card to boost your spirits and know that you can contribute.

This enables you to develop a core sense of self-confidence that you can always come back to.

What does this calling card look like?

Just like some comedians have jokes they are famous for, or someone is known to be acerbic and sharp, or someone's humor is hilariously dark, it starts with asking yourself what your strengths and skills are.

This is a general question.

This does not necessarily have to be specific to social interaction. Now that you are aware of your strengths and skills, the next step is to focus on social situations. What are your strengths and skills in relation to social situations?

What are the moments you remember that things went well for you? It might be the jokes you made or the overall tone of the conversation.

Do people laugh when you make observations or self-deprecating jokes? Do they react well when you're genuine, authentic, and emotional? What about when you are flippant and irreverent? Do you formulate questions in an oddball way? Do you have funny views on particular topics? Do you have a couple of great stories about crazy experiences? Do you role-play well, or do funny voices?

You might think that you're terrible at everything I've mentioned and have no redeeming skills, but everyone has (1) great social experiences in their lifetimes, and (2) social strengths.

Take out a sheet of paper and identify these.

Once you have clearly identified your social strengths, when you're down always go back to this calling card. You now think that you're the type of person that can have successes and triumphs, and be confident in some areas.

Draw your strength from this. It's a starting point – a small slice of the social pie that you feel you have mastered, are untouchable in, and can display in front of anyone.

It's important to keep practicing these special social gifts that you already have. Eventually, you'll become known as the "go-to" person for certain types of questions, analysis, opinions, or just simple assurance. Maybe you can be known as a person who's a great listener. Whatever the case is, you develop the positive social skills that you already have.

**Become a Teacher**

Think about the last time someone came to you for help, and how confident you felt when you were teaching them.

When you become skilled enough, or are simply the person who can provide help to others, that is a massive social advantage.

There is an inherent power differential created that instantly puts you on a pedestal of sorts. When you feel that people are hanging onto your every word and trying to absorb them, you will rise to the occasion and make them look at you differently and respect you more.

For example, how do you feel when people ask you for directions in your own neighborhood? You feel a measure of confidence because you know what you're talking about, and someone is asking for guidance.

So look for opportunities where you can teach others in a social situation.

It might be about an obscure concept that comes up in conversation or how to correctly pour a beer. These are the types of things that create social cachet for you and give you great feedback from others that will build your confidence step by step.

To emphasize, confidence takes work and may not come naturally.

You are trying to overcome habits you've carried for a long time. Don't think that just because you've resolved to make a change things will fall into place quickly.

Take the time to educate yourself and become an expert in the things that you are already good at or for which you get praised – your calling cards.

If you want more social confidence, do it in areas concerning social situations and conversations that involve your expertise. Start in an area you know you can succeed in and slowly branch out. Set small goals, exceed them, and build confidence in knowing that you are growing better and better.

Once you achieve your initial goals, start expanding on those goals and keep surpassing them. Keep raising the bar until you're no longer good at simple dark jokes, but great at talking to people through a dark sense of humor and so on.

Your confidence will grow in an incremental way, brick by brick, until is a towering wall. It begins with your skills.

## Chapter 6. How to be "In The Zone" for Any Social Situation

It's time for me to come right out and say it.

I'm no spring chicken anymore. I'm not old, but physically I'm not the spry and limber 21-year old personal trainer I once was.

This all came to a head last year when I walked into the gym, and without warming up or stretching, started squatting heavy weights. Normally the story would go that I walked out of the gym a while later, tired but feeling good. That's not what happened. I couldn't walk out of the gym at all. I had sprained my medial collateral ligament (MCL) and needed crutches for the next month.

Guess who learned a hard lesson about warming up and stretching?

We do this in all aspects of our lives where we have to perform and/or be evaluated. We make sure our head is on straight, our muscles are activated, and our game faces are on.

Public speakers and singers go through elaborate routines and mental steps to allow them to get into the zone physically and mentally. Athletes obviously warm up their muscles before any type of competition.

Why not do the same with social confidence and social situations?

The *not-so-secret* secret to social confidence is preparation.

Compare this to the typical social situation where you aren't prepared and you aren't warmed up.

Someone comes over to say hello to you and the words out of your mouth are muddled and unsure because you were in your own world and your vocal cords were rusty. You probably have to clear your throat and cough before you can even respond.

What do you talk about with this person? What did they say? You can't even remember what you did over the weekend. Wait, what did I do earlier today? How *was* it?

You're completely caught off-guard that you can't even remember what you did that weekend, much less earlier that day.

When you fail to prepare, you come in with low confidence that gets dragged even lower by a lukewarm reception from others. You'll create a downward spiral where perceived negative impressions work with your own self-doubt and low self-esteem to make you feel downright lousy.

With that said, it's also very important to understand that preparation can only take you so far. It's helpful, but not a permanent fix. For some, that's all that is needed to get into the correct state of mind. For others, this is a misleading boost that wears off quickly or at the fist sign of discomfort or failure. Even so, preparation can be very helpful.

Here are some methods to warm up your social confidence so you can walk into any room ready with a presence.

**Social Warm-Up Exercise #1: Read 300 words out loud.**

Preferably, pick an excerpt from a children's book that includes dialogue from a few very different characters. Pretend you're an elementary school teacher reading a story to your kids. Try to express as much emotion in your narration as you can. Use different voices. For example, you should scream, whisper, laugh loudly, and exaggerate everything.

Do this at least three times, and you'll notice a huge difference between the first and the third reading. That's because you're more emotionally expressive.

Use the facial expressions that each emotion takes and exaggerate them to the tenth degree – wide eyes, inquisitive eyebrows, huge pouts, enormous smiles, and engaged expressions.

This will warm your voice up and increase your baseline of

what's socially acceptable. When you can easily scream the goofy voice of a cartoon eggplant, suddenly you'll feel more capable and free in social situations.

This also reminds you of the wide range of emotional expressions you're capable of in a social situation. When you do this, it also has a physical effect. You raise your heart rate and it pumps adrenaline throughout your system. You start social interactions warm in every sense.

**Social Warm-Up Exercise #2: Visualize the social situation you'll be getting into.**

Visualization is seeing yourself in the third person as if you are watching from a seat in a movie theater.

Pretend that you are watching yourself in action. Watch yourself go through each of the situations that you are not sure about and watch yourself do well in all of them. When you visualize, imagine what it looks like to perform flawlessly in a social situation.

Try to imagine every little detail and think through it, and watch yourself perform them. What parts were you prepared for, and which were you unprepared for?

The reason this works is because our lack of social confidence of stems from our sense that social situations are unpredictable.

We feel things are so unpredictable that we give into assuming we're just going to crash and burn because we're unprepared. By going through visualization exercises, you make the unpredictable predictable. You do this by watching the scene play out again and again and again. This way, when things take an unexpected turn, you will be ready.

Even if you are not exactly ready for it, at least you have some pivot options available to you. Compare this to simply getting caught unaware. With visualization, you are less likely to freak out when things spiral unpredictably.

**Social Warm-Up Exercise #3: Use external stimuli.**

Regardless of which method you pick, make sure that it increases your heart rate and gets your adrenaline pumped up – that is the main goal. When you literally feel your body warmed up, you feel more alert and quick mentally.

Some people respond well to music, while others require something a little bit more physical like doing push-ups, jogging in place, or jumping up and down.

Other people are more auditory and prefer inspiring speeches. Some people like reading inspirational quotes about social interactions and social mastery. Whatever gets you inspired, do it.

Everybody is different when it comes to external stimuli. Just figure out what kind of external stimuli gets you pumped up and go for it. The most common combination is peppy music with jumping jacks or push-ups – at least, for me.

**Social Warm-Up Exercise #4: Create index cards with**

**confidence anchors.**

As I've mentioned, you should have a mental calling card. It's your reminder to yourself that you are good at certain things. And by remembering these qualities, you allow yourself to feel good about them.

For this warm up, I want you to do this physically.

On an index card, write down your five greatest moments – the ones when you were completely social; the five times you were in the social zone where you smoothly interacted with people without effort or anxiety. Write down the names of the five people who make you feel the most social along with your five best social experiences.

Carry this card around at all times to remind you of the kind of person you are. By reading these notes, you summon those memories and emotions. You benefit from the surge of emotional and mental engagement that you get, and you get psyched up for what lies ahead.

It just makes too much sense to be ready for social interaction when you know it's coming. Start your days off on the right foot, and you'll start to notice that you have many more good days than bad.

# Chapter 7. Taking Action Against Insecurity

To a certain degree, most people are self-aware.

For those who lack social confidence, it's almost the opposite problem – they are *too* aware and assume everyone makes the same judgments as they do.

Most people have a relatively clear idea about the sources of their insecurity. You might feel that you don't dress well, you stutter when you speak, and you can't approach new people. Even having a rough idea of your insecurities can be important.

But simply having that knowledge doesn't make a difference.

What is the missing ingredient?

Huge, immediate action. You need to do something about it and take the bull by the horns to minimize your sources of social insecurity.

If you stay in your head and continually analyze your insecurities and shortcomings in lieu of action, you might just be stuck forever. Many people who lack social confidence and have social anxiety are stuck because they prefer to spin their wheels and are afraid to take action.

It's one of the comforting aspects of analysis paralysis – you never have to do anything when you're endlessly evaluating your course of action.

Not all action has to be as scary as walking into a room full of strangers and striking up conversation. This chapter focuses on understanding the low-hanging causes of your lack of social confidence and shoring them up so you will have less to worry about.

We lack social confidence because we feel we are inadequate in certain areas of our lives. It's time to start doing something about that – actively – and tackle the low-hanging fruit to minimize sources of your insecurity.

Rather than ask you to articulate the Pandora's Box of your biggest social insecurities, I have three ways for you to minimize your insecurities, starting one by one.

Even if you start with a hundred insecurities and manage to eliminate only one, that's one less thing you have to worry about. The longer you choose not to resolve or work on your insecurities, the longer your insecurities will continue to drag you down.

Keep in mind that just because you reduce the number of

insecurities you have, this doesn't magically mean that all your problems will go away. We can be confident in 99% of what we do, but if that 1% arises, we freeze.

Sometimes it takes only the smallest thing to knock us down. So, it's really about resolving to eliminate as many of these insecurities as possible. The more you eliminate, the better you will make things for yourself.

Don't get stuck in self-pity thinking about your lack of social confidence, be proactive and solution oriented.

It's always an incremental process and we're starting it right now. Can you decide to make things happen today?

Of course, we're all different and we all bring our unique, personal spin to these three general groupings. But as unique as your situations may be, I guarantee that if you look at them closely enough, you can generalize them to fall into one of these three categories.

**You are insecure about your presentation.**

You might think that this is pandering to people, but that's just the way the world works.

Sorry.

People do judge books by their covers. You can complain and whine all you want about how this should not be the case—but hey, living in reality is all about focusing on how things actually are and not obsessing about how things should be. While you can try to change people's minds and assumptions, you still have to deal with the reality on the ground.

Your presentation is getting in the way of your social confidence. There's no way around it. You are either not feeling good about yourself and it shows, or you are dressing and carrying yourself in a way that causes other people to pre-judge you – which we know creates a lukewarm reception that you will probably notice.

Luckily, this is the easiest category to change. It's about carrying yourself with better posture and asking a friend of the opposite sex how they would groom and dress you better.

When you look good, you feel good, and other people feel good about being around someone that feels good. Did you get that?

When it comes to your physical presentation, you don't have to become a makeup queen, male or female. The 80-20 rule holds very strong here – 20% of your efforts should generate about 80% of the presentation transformation or upgrade you need to feel great about yourself.

At first, it might feel as if you're wearing a costume. But hey – the old you wasn't doing your social confidence any favors, was it?

The bottom line is to just give a damn about this, and realize that it's a huge part of the equation – one that others seem to naturally manage. It's actually highly manufactured with lots of effort.

**You are insecure about running out of things to say or afraid of saying something stupid.**

If you are self-conscious and worried that people will judge you if you say something stupid or "off," there's an easy workaround to that.

The best approach is simple preparation.

Create answers to predictable questions and conversations. Run that mental videotape in your mind about your past 10, 20, or 30 social conversations. I guarantee they are not all that different from each other.

All social conversations, especially among total strangers, tend to follow certain predictable patterns. It's very, very rare that you will have a really deep, profound, existential, and philosophically-rich conversation with somebody you don't know from Adam.

While it does happen, those conversations are rare pieces of brain candy. For the most part, our social conversations tend to be fairly shallow. Use this to your advantage.

Since you know there are only so many directions a typical conversation in a light social setting will take, be proactive. Figure out the general questions that people will ask and the topics that will come up in normal conversation and be prepared with story-answers.

For example,

How was your weekend?
What are you doing this weekend?
How was your day?
What do you do for work?

The key is to realize that these questions are just people's attempts to hear something interesting and not actually requests for literal answers, mundane answers. You can think about these beforehand, and simply by being prepared, you will freak out less.

Instead of feeling intimidated and scared, by thinking through these kinds of questions and your answers ahead of time, you gain confidence knowing that you will perform well because you have rehearsed your answers.

Predictability is the foundation to social comfort. If you want to be comfortable in any kind of social setting, even if you are dealing with complete and total strangers, look for predictable patterns.

**Target other specific insecurities, isolate them and think of ways to improve them by 10%**

You're not trying to completely eliminate *all* your social insecurities. That's tough work. But focusing on improving just 10% of them is manageable and will boost your social confidence.

If you put too much pressure on yourself by trying to tackle 100% of your social insecurities at once, you'll probably fail and become even more discouraged than when you started.

That's the value of focusing on small, incremental changes.

So what are some specific insecurities you can isolate and think about improving in the social context?

Maybe you're insecure when certain topics come up, or about how much money you make, or the school you went to. Maybe you hate having to talk about yourself, tell stories, or answer questions. Or perhaps you hate talking to strangers.

By simply choosing to improve these areas of insecurity by making small changes, you will eventually end up realizing dramatic improvements. Think in terms of baby steps. Don't think in terms of gigantic global changes. Those kinds of gigantic changes are definitely more than welcome, but they also take a lot more work and you will be better off starting small.

They are also more likely to lead to backsliding so that you end up where you started. If you don't want that to happen, focus on taking baby steps because these will increase the likelihood that whatever changes you make will be permanent.

# Chapter 8. Is it Clinical?

It's time a take a deeper look into the problem of the lack of social confidence.

There's an objectively acceptable level of anxiety and stress associated with social situations that we all experience – even me.

But once that anxiety starts interfering with your ability to live your life, or when you are spending hours fixating over a two-minute interaction, things have reached a level that is objectively unacceptable.

That's when you need to start looking into real, clinical definitions of social anxiety, social anxiety disorder, or general anxiety disorder to see if your symptoms merit professional help.

The good news about social anxiety is that it is fairly easy to identify. You are suffering from social anxiety if you suffer from behavioral, mental, and physical symptoms related to social situations. They are all intertwined.

What does this look like?

On a physical level, people might experience a rapid heart rate. They might shake or even rock their body as if trying to comfort themselves. Some people break out in a cold sweat or feel slightly nauseous. Some develop dry mouth. As trying as the physical symptoms are, the real action takes place mentally.

On a mental level, people with social anxiety are often paralyzed with fear or are so distracted and worried that they really can't figure much of anything out. This can build up to such an extent it will be reflected in their behavior.

What common behavior do people suffering from social anxiety exhibit?

They want to physically escape from social situations that make them feel ill at ease. Also, when they do end up interacting with people, they tend to stumble over their words, stutter, or continually loop back and talk about the same things over and over again. Worst of all, you can quickly tell that they'd rather be anywhere else than be in that conversation.

Remember that there are completely natural levels of anxiety's impact on you, so you have to determine where you fall on that spectrum.

The worst effect of social anxiety is its social impact on you. Human beings are social animals. You avoid situations and people you shouldn't be avoiding – people that can make you feel better. Being cut off from social validation and encouragement is the biggest toll social anxiety imposes. You feel isolated and stranded on an island.

People with real social anxiety practice a lot of avoidance. They know that certain social settings trigger anxiety so they go completely out of their way to avoid those situations. This kind of behavior follows a fairly simply logic: when you're in social situations, this happens and you feel terrible. If you don't get into those situations, then this doesn't happen and you feel just fine.

The list of situations grows expansive over time and starts to harm your long-term interests in every area of your life. You let your social avoidance and social fears dictate how you live your life, and that serves no one.

The worst manifestation of this social avoidance behavior is that you end up arranging your life into lonely, sterile, unproductive, and unfulfilling routines. Avoidance can make people miss out on large, important parts of life because they're trying to prevent themselves from ever feeling uncomfortable. You may feel safe because you've exempted yourself from social interactions that intimidate or scare you, but you're stagnating.

People can partially avoid avoidance situations through safety and coping behaviors. A safety behavior is something a person does that allows them to be in an anxiety-provoking situation, but that shelters them from the full brunt of whatever it is they're afraid of.

For example, when someone goes to a party and he is scared to death of big crowds, he might want to drink a lot as a safety behavior. This compensates his otherwise default tendency to just avoid the effect of that social situation by not showing up. Instead, this person shows up but drinks more alcohol than he should.

Overall, coping and safety behaviors are unhealthy and do nothing to solve the cause of the problems, only the manifestations and symptoms.

If you're reading this and thinking that sounds like you, or that all sounds like fairly normal behavior, then it's time to dive even deeper into the differences between merely lacking social confidence and what might border on a mental illness.

While it may feel crippling and debilitating as far as your social interactions go, the clinical definition of social anxiety is very different.

These are crippling phobias that blow away whatever shyness you may have. A phobia is where you outright lose the ability to function because of your fear. It's the nightmare you have when you wake up drenched with sweat.

That is a mental condition.

If you notice that you are quite uncomfortable with people because you have a lot of social anxiety, don't assume this means you're crazy. A normal person without much social confidence might attend a party and generally stay in the corner until spoken to. But someone with true social anxiety might go to the party and feel as if they want to vomit, or start shaking, or be drenched in sweat from head to toe, or exhibit any number of other extreme responses.

So what is the clinical definition of social anxiety?

According to the DSM-5, which is the official standardized guide of mental disorders as published by the American Psychiatric Association, social anxiety disorder is:

"**A**. *Marked fear or anxiety about one or more social situations in which the individual is exposed to possible scrutiny by others. Examples include social interactions (e.g., having a conversation, meeting unfamiliar people), being observed (e.g., eating or drinking), and performing in front of others (e.g., giving a speech).*

**B.** *The individual fears that he or she will act in a way or show anxiety symptoms that will be negatively evaluated (i.e., will be humiliating and embarrassing; will lead to rejection or offend others).*

**C.** *The social situations almost always provoke fear or anxiety.*

**D.** *The social situations are avoided or endured with intense fear or anxiety.*

**E.** *The fear or anxiety is out of proportion to the actual threat posed by the social situation and to the sociocultural context.*

*G. The fear, anxiety, or avoidance causes clinically significant distress or impairment in social, occupational, or other important areas of functioning."*

If you fit these definitions, does this mean you're going crazy? No.

You just have issues to work on. It's important to understand how this all plays out.

The worst part is that it creates a spiral of misery.

They are unhappy about their condition. They are unhappy about how they respond to social settings. They feel isolated and powerless and hopeless. They feel shame because they can't manage to overcome something that seems to come so easily to so many people.

Here are some common situations that people with true social anxiety might react to in a way that isn't objectively acceptable, and might be clinical in nature.

There might be significant distress in the following seemingly normal situations:

- Meeting new people
- Being criticized or teased
- Being the center of attention or having to tell stories
- Being aware that you are being watched as if in a performance
- Meeting people in "authority"
- Being called on in class
- Speaking or presenting in front of others

- Asking for something or making a request
- Giving their (honest) opinion about something
- Making eye contact
- Any potentially confrontational situation
- Deviating into personal topics
- Awkward situations
- Asking for a correction on their order in a restaurant

One of the most common treatments for true social anxiety is cognitive behavioral therapy (CBT).

Even though the next chapter focuses on actionable techniques for both social confidence and social anxiety, it's a good idea to have a clear overview of the wide range of treatments available.

CBT consists of two portions. The first is more akin to traditional therapy where you discuss your problems with a licensed therapist, and you attempt to dispel the assumptions and past experiences that have led you to crippling social anxiety.

When we continue to have irrational thoughts, eventually they crowd out rational thinking and we develop negative mental habits that can infect every area of our life.

This portion of CBT goes a long way in unraveling a lot of the assumptions we may have about ourselves. This is definitely a great approach to overcoming negative mental habits. We end up relearning how we should respond to social triggers and unlearning harmful habits. In a sense, it's like a class where you learn about the causes and try to identify them in yourself.

The second component is the behavior modification.

In this component, people voluntarily put themselves in situations that may cause mild anxiety.

They then start becoming used to the situation and practice a lot of the cognitive reprogramming they have learned on a step by step basis. With enough repetition and enough time, cognitive behavioral therapy can help resolve social anxiety disorder without resorting to brain altering chemicals like anti-anxiety medications.

Only a change in the brain's neural pathways can cause permanent changes to occur so that we can change irrational thinking into rational thinking and then act on it.

## Chapter 9. Slaying the Dragon

The previous chapter was an overview of true social anxiety and just how crippling it can be.

Where along the spectrum do you lie?

Regardless, in this chapter, we'll go over techniques you can use to take control over yourself in social situations. They are in the same vein as the behavioral component of CBT, and I will take you step by step to deal with the problems through what's known as exposure therapy.

Getting over social anxiety is easier said than done. It's easy to say, "Today, I am going to finally get over my problem." Change almost never occurs without some level of discomfort. You need to be ready for the discomfort that any necessary change inevitably brings to the table.

No pain, no gain.

Getting over social anxiety involves breaking the association between social situations, and your fears and anxiety. You're trying to break the link between certain triggers that you see and the past behavioral pattern that you automatically fall into.

When you properly expose yourself to your social fears, you'll learn that you don't have much to fear. You also gain the understanding that the negative outcomes aren't really all that bad. In many cases, they are completely nonexistent.

The second thing you'll realize when you voluntarily expose yourself to your social fears is that you are always in control. When you fear social failure or awkward moments, those moments happen because you contribute to such situations.

For example, if you're already thinking that an upcoming social event will feel awkward and be personally disappointing, if not downright uncomfortable, what do you think will happen?

You will start behaving in such a way that people will react to you exactly the way you've anticipated they will react. Your fears and expectations become a self-fulfilling prophecy. This is an important thing to remember when you begin to put yourself in social situations that trigger fear and anxiety.

One thing we need to get out of the way right now is the idea that when you decide to get over your social anxiety your fears will somehow magically disappear; that given enough time and effort, your social fears will simply vaporize. Unfortunately, there's a good chance they will never entirely go away. But that doesn't mean there isn't a lot you can do to make things easier on yourself.

Instead of hoping to do away with your fears completely, a more realistic approach is to focus more on managing them properly and subduing them to a degree that you can handle. This will allow you to enjoy social situations.

If you shoot for simply managing them properly, you will have achieved quite a bit indeed. The important thing here is to take the step of facing your fear and not getting your heart set on a specific outcome.

This is where exposure therapy comes in.

Exposure therapy is where you take small, incremental, and gradual steps to expose yourself to your social fears in varying ways related to your main fear.

Take a tiny aspect of the fear, and turn what seems like a giant leap of faith into a mild step that makes you feel safer so that you can take the next mild step.

You're aiming to make incremental improvements – not to leap forward with abandon and just hope things will dramatically improve overnight.

What you're also doing by taking mild steps is giving your definition of success a fighting chance. Experiencing failure after failure because you've aimed too high will work against you.  But when you've enjoyed success after success because you've set reachable goals, your self-esteem will increase and each new situation will bring you further success and confidence.

For example, if *every* kind of social interaction makes you uncomfortable, you might want to start by simply allowing yourself to smile at strangers more often. It's a relatively small step that can be accomplished very quickly – all it takes is one second.

Commit to smiling at a strange once a day.  That's all it takes to begin.

In most cases, they will repay your smile with a smile of their own. Now, that wasn't so horrible, was it?

Once you have accomplished this small step, you can move on to saying hello or waving to people as a form of social pleasantry. Each step you take builds on the last. What's important is to start with gradual exposure and take baby steps forward.

**Situation #1: Doing the action you fear, but in an easier or less intense situation.**

Suppose that you experience anxiety about speaking to new people.

If that's the case with you, you'll want to try speaking with someone you don't know, but in an easy, safe, and non-threatening circumstance.

A good example of this would be chatting up the barista at

your favorite coffee bar, or the cashier at the market, or any service personnel that is attending to you. They are accustomed to making small talk with customers, so they will help make it easy for you – and the encounter carries no risk because nothing is at stake. Even better, it will be short. It will only last as long as your credit card takes to swipe, and that's a relief for most.

Speak to a barista or cashier for one or two more sentences than you normally would. Ask how they are and what they are doing this weekend. Ask if the store has been busy. Ask if they have had the food or coffee that you are ordering and what they think about it.

Ask a stranger for the time, or easy directions.

Do this once every other day, and you'll be off to a great start.

You're still doing the same basic action you fear, but you are choosing your battles better to increase the chances that you'll walk away with a more positive outcome and a successful notch on your belt.

**Situation #2: Do something similar to the situation you fear that brings up the same feelings.**

Let's take the same example and say your anxiety is speaking to strangers.

What happens to you in this situation? You might feel anxious, stressed, your palms sweat and you stumble over your words.

What situations are similar to having to speak to strangers?

Some examples could be opening a door for someone, riding up in an elevator with someone, having to call a customer service number to ask a question, playing a team sport, or even chatting in an anonymous Internet chat room.

Whatever the case, allow yourself to engage in different social interactions while feeling the same tension as your desired goal.

**Situation #3: Practice the exact thing you fear, but in a controlled setting.**

Luckily, there are numerous groups, both social and professional (and clinical!) that exist for this very purpose.

Toastmasters is a great example of this. Toastmasters is essentially a public speaking group where members engage in planned or impromptu speeches, each meant to help the speaker become more comfortable with public speaking and destroy their fears.

If it petrifies you to talk to complete strangers, you can also join social skills groups where you can do exercises together. Everyone there is in the same boat, so there is no judgment, plenty of understanding, and it is a completely safe environment for you.

Finally, you can even engage in role playing or exercise with a trained professional. A therapist can walk you through situations and build your confidence and skills because that is their very purpose.

Again, the important part is that you are in a safe setting. Nobody is going to judge you. Nobody is going to make you feel uncomfortable and awkward.

You know that this is controlled and there will be no unpredictable surprises. This increases the likelihood that you will end up practicing the social interaction over and over again until you are comfortable and a lot of your fears dissipate. It may not go away completely, but at least you can reduce it to a manageable level.

The bottom line is simple: social fear and the lack of social confidence are primarily founded on ignorance and lack of experience.

The good news is that both of these can easily be remedied. Ignorance exists simply because you don't have all the information you need. To remedy that, you must be open minded and allow yourself to be in a wide range of situations so that you will get the information that you need. You can overcome your lack of experience by getting out more often. Accumulating these experiences slowly will help make your fears manageable.

By taking small baby steps, you will go a long way toward finally slaying the dragon of social awkwardness and diminishing the fears that have been holding you back.

# Chapter 10. The Art of Self-Acceptance

One of the core issues with lack of social confidence is that people don't accept themselves as they are.

They see someone else that appears to be flawless and brave in the spotlight and wonder why they can't be like that person. They beat themselves up and hold themselves to arbitrary standards that are unyielding and rigid.

It's much like the way women sometimes fixate on their weight and won't believe a word you have to say when you tell them they look great, even if they only weigh 100 pounds/45 kilograms.

In reality, they might even be just fine in social situations, but they have an extremely low self-image because of the comparisons they draw and the standards they keep.

The standards for success they keep are essentially that of perfection. It's a recipe for perpetually feeling like a failure because they can never win. They subscribe to such a high definition of success that they feel like perpetual failures. For example, even if they acknowledge they can do 99 out of 100 things, for them true success is 100 out of 100 things – perfection that can never be reached.

You are a perfectionist and you have defined yourself out of happiness and self-acceptance.

Definition is the key.

The key to social self-acceptance is to define a realistic and objective expectation of success. No more, no less. Objective means it's good enough for others, and realistic means that it's not about perfection, but the impact you make.

If you examine your personal assumptions closely enough, you will realize there's often a disconnect between your definition of acceptable (subjective) and what *objectively* is acceptable. Doing this doesn't mean that you are lowering your standards and just scraping by.

It's almost always the opposite.

In most cases, you may have raised the bar so high that you are unnecessarily beating yourself up with unrealistic expectations of yourself. This leads to you expecting yourself to perform flawlessly while at the same time you let everyone else slide. You don't give yourself any leeway because you feel you will be harshly judged, and yet you probably don't judge others in the same way.

What can you do? You can split the difference and still

come out ahead.

If an objective day of hard work involves showing up and putting in eight hours of work, doing more than that standard will give you a competitive advantage. If your definition of success is to completely read your boss's mind and master everything there is to know about your work, then you've set the bar too high.

There is quite a bit of space between the bare minimum required by your career and your high expectations.

This is what you should base your self-confidence and self-esteem on, not the imagined ideal that only leads to disappointment.

Another key component of self-acceptance is being able to forgive yourself. This is in contrast to beating yourself up over every little mistake you make.

You can forgive yourself for not being perfect.

Once you can forgive yourself, you can let go, learn, and move on. When you can't muster the ability to forgive yourself, you dwell on your mistakes and begin a downward descent that results in your self-esteem taking a beating.

You can practice self-acceptance and forgiveness without being arrogant, complacent, or too accepting of failure.

One common excuse perfectionists give themselves is that they have to hang on to extremely high standards because any kind of slippage means they are settling or that they are being lazy — or worse, on their way to failing.

This is flawed thinking.

It's about accepting that you are a person who makes mistakes from time to time.

Once you give yourself a bit of room to make a mistake from time to time, you will recognize that mistakes are opportunities to learn and improve.

The improvement might not be immediately perceptible, but it's there. It's a process. And in that process, you'll grow and move that much closer to where you want to be as far as your confidence and happiness go.

One of the best ways to fully accept yourself is to celebrate your strengths.

You may have been beating yourself up for so long that you have convinced yourself that you have no redeeming values.

That is absolutely not true. Maybe you're a lousy singer, but you're a great basketball player. Maybe you have punctuality issues and are always late for work but you write better reports than anyone in your office. Maybe you are sometimes slow to reach the right conclusion or make the best decision, but you are meticulous in the way you approach problems and your end result is always good.

Whatever the case, no one is a complete and total failure or has no value. We all have our strengths. Maybe our weaknesses vastly outnumber our strengths, but that doesn't diminish our strengths.

Don't take these for granted.

List them out.

Acknowledge them regardless of how minor or inconsequential they may seem to you. Allow yourself to feel good about the fact that you possess these strengths. Actively practice gratitude for what you have in your life and what you're capable of.

If you have a tough time counting your blessings and celebrating your strengths, you might want to try volunteering to see the spectrum of suffering.

Regardless of how you do it, I guarantee you will walk away with a fresh perspective and a new appreciation for your life and your worth.

You might see yourself as trash because you're stuck in your middle management job. You might think that you're not as respected as you should be. But guess what, the vast majority of people out there have it worse than you do.

You allowed yourself to be blind to just how rich, how talented, and how valuable you are as a person.

Perhaps the most important aspect of self-acceptance is to stop being a slave to your ideals.

According to prominent psychologist Ryan Howes, "Many of

our problems with self-acceptance come from our inability to reconcile who we are as compared with the idealized dreams of our youth."

Whatever your dreams and goals may be, give them a proper burial and mourn them. Allow yourself to feel sad for that one time those dreams and ideals did not come to pass.

Once you're done with mourning, get back to being the best you can possibly be. That's all you can do. There's really no other way.

By allowing yourself to be enslaved by grandiose dreams of the past that for some reason or other did not materialize, you're just holding back the greatness that you could possibly be enjoying in the here and now. Live more for the present by focusing on what exists now, instead of getting all worked up about how things should be or could have been.

The world only rewards results. It could not care less about what you could've done, should've done, or would've done. By accepting your strengths and focusing on what needs to be done now, you put yourself on the road to stronger self-esteem and complete self-acceptance.

## Chapter 11. Toxic, Draining Habits

In this chapter, I'm going to spell out what you should *not* do if you are looking to increase your social confidence. This chapter is about behaviors you are most likely engaging in that you need to stop. These are behaviors that people who lack social confidence consistently do.

They can't help it because they don't know any better.

A client of mine was the quintessential example of someone who cannot handle compliments. He never quite believed that people were telling the truth. He just couldn't accept that people had a decent opinion of him.

So what did he do whenever he received a compliment, no matter how small?

He denied forcefully and demanded people to stop lying to him. He would become visibly livid and start shaking at the thought that someone would dare do that to him when he was just trying to live his life. It wasn't helping him socially, to say the least.

That's the first toxic habit you need to eliminate.

**Accepting Compliments**

Start allowing yourself to graciously accept compliments from other people – and don't be afraid to compliment or praise yourself.

People with low social confidence can't handle genuine compliments well because they have such a negative self-image. When something conflicts with their mental picture of themselves and of their capabilities, they automatically believe the other person is putting them on.

Believe it or not, you do have traits that people find admirable.

Do this instead: *believe them*. They're not yanking your chain or setting you up for a big joke.

If somebody is genuinely complimenting you, believe them, acknowledge them, and thank them. As long as they are sincere, then you need to believe them and you need to remember that compliment.

Begin with the belief and assumption that people find you valuable. This is evidence to combat the assumptions that negatively drain you.

Write them down and remember them. The next time you feel down about a situation, look at the compliment list and remember *that's* the type of person you really are.

## Constant Comparisons

We've already talked about how toxic comparisons are part of the behavior of those with low social confidence.

In a nutshell, comparing yourself to others' skills in something you have no reason to excel at only makes you question your own worth.

Moreover, you're almost always comparing the best, public version of that other person and failing to recognize that they have their own internal struggles. And, you're comparing their best moment with your worst moment. It's not even apples to oranges; it's a steak to computers.

You have no way of winning. Stop beating yourself up with unnecessary comparisons.

Put another way, it's like comparing someone's social media feed of all the amazing restaurants they've eaten at the microwaved lunches you have at work.

## Fixating on (perceived) failures

It's easy to understand why people are fixated on their failures.

Our failures are impactful and emotional, yet we take many of our daily victories and talents for granted.

There's a normal, baseline level of focusing on your failures

– this is natural because no one wants to repeat them, so some attention to them is due.

But when you fixate on them to the point of fear and a crippling lack of confidence, you ignore all your other victories in that arena and let your failures write your disempowering narrative.

If you allow yourself to dwell on your failures, eventually even your neutral experiences will start to look like failures. That's a perceived failure.

Look at failures for what they truly are. They are a valuable list of instructions for how not to fail in the future.

Thomas Edison once said that he didn't fail to invent the light bulb. He just succeeded in finding 10,000 ways that didn't work.

You can look at failure as a paralyzing experience that permeates your life with fear or just as a to-do list of items you can work on to achieve better results. Think of it as a not-to-do list for future reference.

Instead of fixating on your failures, allot equal mind space to positivity and your victories. Give your victories and positivity equal time. Make a rule to think about the times you succeeded whenever you think about your failures and perceived failures.

**Sweating the small stuff**

This occurs when we relate everything going wrong in our

lives to one of our perceived inadequacies.

For example, if you did not get that promotion at work, you might just sum it all up by saying, "Well, it's because I'm a bad person and worthless at work."

Not small stuff?

What about having your self-worth take a deep dive because of a small side comment someone made about your contribution to a project, a comment which was patently false.

The negative self-talk you give yourself in response is unhealthy and inaccurate.

Often, minor comments aren't even a judgment on you – they are merely observations made by other people. There is no malice and no slight on your character. You are the only one who heard it that way. So stop thinking that minor things mean some sort of extremely negative judgment on your character or capabilities.

Know the difference between a quirk and a true character flaw.

Try to let things go and bask in what went right in your day. Focus on the things that went smoothly. Resist trying to equate positives and negatives at the end of the day. If anything, the negatives are just minor details. They are 1-2 pages in a rich chapter of 100 pages.

In most cases, the negatives are temporary setbacks that

really don't mean all that much in the big scheme of things. Try to keep perspective.

## Making Excuses

When you make excuses, you are lying to yourself.

You might not realize it because your defense mechanisms are so strong, but you're telling yourself that you would take action *but for* the following ....When in reality, it's not something you even intended to do because you were too scared of it.

When you make excuses for yourself, you're enabling your lack of social confidence to grow. Moreover, you are teaching yourself subconsciously that you can't and won't take action.

People often try to justify their fear in such a way that it prevents any future progress from ever happening. When you're making constant excuses to avoid taking action, you're simply cementing learned helplessness. You end up putting yourself in a position where you just cannot fix the situation.

Instead, be honest and upfront with yourself about why you don't want to do something.

It's okay to say that you're just afraid. Actually, it's empowering to be so honest with yourself and finally understand what you're facing. Because then you can start to fix it.

On the other hand, if you subscribe to a grand theory as to why you can't take action at that very moment, you're just hypnotizing yourself to even more pronounced levels of helplessness.

## Living in an Echo Chamber

An echo chamber is where you can only hear yourself and your own opinion. There are no dissenting thoughts because... it's an echo chamber. Everything you hear will be in agreement with you.

Your friends can function like echo chambers, unfortunately. Some of them prefer to be, actually.

But if you are in an echo chamber of low confidence and negativity, imagine what happens when you bring your troubles into the fold. Everyone agrees with you, enables you, and generally tells you that you are right, that you don't need to change, and that it's not your fault.

I know birds of a feather flock together, but if you want to soar like an eagle you better stop hanging around with turkeys.

If you tell your friends your excuses and they accept them, you have the wrong friends. You're in an echo chamber.

Real friends want the best for you. And sometimes, that means telling you the harsh reality of what needs to change, or what you are really doing. They don't enable you, they are simply honest and don't always validate your excuses.

That's how real friendship works.

A lot of people mistake friendship as some sort of emotional codependency where you enable each other's deficiencies and limiting beliefs, and drag each other down. That is not a productive friendship.

A real friend is an honest friend. As long as you agree to certain rules of communication that govern the expression of uncomfortable truths, your friends can help you live up to your fullest potential and get out of your negative emotional spirals regarding your self-acceptance and self-esteem.

With your existing friends, your task is simple. Seek more honesty from them.

Tell them "Tell me straight out what you really think."

If you can't handle straight talk, maybe you can lay out some ground rules so you can still get the straight facts but delivered in such a way that they won't crush your self-esteem unnecessarily. Another thing you can do is seek out new friends you know are blunt and honest. Whatever the case, you need more honesty in your life if you detect that you live in an echo chamber of excuses.

# Chapter 12. Social Confidence Perspectives

At this point, it will be useful to hear a philosophy on social confidence that isn't mine.

There are far more qualified people to talk about the subject, and I've compiled their approaches verbatim in this chapter to provide you with additional perspectives on how to face any social situation head on.

These quotes contain extremely powerful truths that can help you overcome your self-esteem and social confidence issues. There are many ways to interpret these quotes, but I've distilled their main points as far as they address self-acceptance, self-esteem, and self-confidence issues.

**"Too many people overvalue what they are not, and undervalue what they are." — Malcolm Forbes**

Forbes zeroes in on the fact that we often reach for things that we shouldn't really care about.

We see this in toxic behaviors such as comparing and being thrown off by small criticisms. We see an ideal that we want to strive for without even thinking about whether it fits what we want, and who we are. Or even whether it should matter to us.

In doing so, we denigrate and devalue the best parts of our lives. We do this by tricking ourselves into thinking that we're trying to improve ourselves. In fact, we're achieving the precise opposite: we end up beating ourselves up unnecessarily.

Focus on what you have and build on that. Stop wasting time, energy, and emotional resources on trying to become another person when you can simply focus on being the best person you are right now.

What if you just focused on valuing your own strengths?

**"Thousands of geniuses live and die undiscovered—either by themselves or by others." — Mark Twain.**

You do yourself a big disservice by not recognizing who you are and what's special about you.

Many children grew up in households where they were conditioned to think that any kind of self-celebration or self-acknowledgement is a form of pride or bragging. I know because that was my childhood household.

It might not be in your nature to brag about yourself or even think about yourself as special and noteworthy. That doesn't mean that you aren't objectively great in your own way.

Alternatively, some people grew up in settings where it seemed that everybody was more accomplished than they were. Maybe you live in a family where there are a couple of millionaires, one or two award-winning scientists, and several high-powered attorneys.

You might think that whatever you achieve in your life will pale in comparison to the achievements of the people who have gone before you, or among your peers. This is another situation that leads you to completely ignore your own achievements.

Both of these comparisons destroy your overall level of confidence and make you dependent on others for feelings of validation and discovery of your genius.

Does that sound like a good way to live? Allow yourself to celebrate yourself. Allow yourself to feel happy.

As the old saying goes, "It's very hard to love others when you cannot even love yourself." You can only give what you have. Stop comparing and allow yourself to discover your inner genius. It is simply an act of self-acknowledgement and self-empowerment. Nobody's going to do it for you.

**"Whether you think you can or you think you can't—you are right." — Henry Ford**

Whatever we believe, we achieve.

In the case of people with low self-esteem and low self-confidence, whatever we believe we can't do we end up not doing. You are constantly programming yourself. Think of your body as a computer and your mind as software. Whatever you choose to voluntarily install in your life's personal computer, you will become.

If I bought two computers and in one only installed software that did photo processing and in the other installed only social media marketing software, the first computer would just be a photo processor and the second would only be good for media marketing. Although each computer would function very differently, the thing to keep in mind is that the hardware on each would be the same. The big difference between them exists because of the software I choose to put in them.

Your life is a self-fulfilling prophecy. Your choice of mental software dictates the shape, reach, and influence of your life. Choose carefully. A lot of the things that seem impossible to you right now are impossible precisely because you've chosen to let them be impossible.

Only your approach to life determines what you can and will achieve. Don't be self-limiting and don't be your own worst enemy.

There was once an eagle that was raised among pigeons. He believed he was a pigeon along with all the limitations of a pigeon. His pigeon family was extremely scared of hawks and always hid when they saw them. One day a hawk swooped toward his pigeon family but flew off immediately as soon as he caught sight of the eagle.

The eagle had no idea who he was and what he was capable of; he was a prisoner of his own lack of belief.

**"Someone else's opinion of you doesn't have to become your reality." — Les Brown**

At the end of the day, the world has its own agenda.

But why should that affect what you do and want?

If doesn't ultimately matter what others say about you. It only matters the moment you start believing them. The moment you start incorporating other people's opinions of you, they'll matter. Otherwise, up to that point, it doesn't really matter.

What truly matters is how you view yourself – that is your personal reality.

People with low social self-confidence often allow the negative perceptions of others to infect their view of themselves.

Everybody else can provide an opinion, but it will only remain an opinion and fail to become your personal reality if you choose not to believe them. Be a more conscientious gatekeeper of your self-esteem. Don't be too quick to let others' negativity or negative views of you infect how you view yourself.

After all, what compels others to be negative or nasty to you? It's almost always about them, not you.

**"I am convinced all of humanity is born with more gifts than we know, most are born geniuses and just get de-geniused rapidly." — Buckminster Fuller**

We're all capable of degrees of greatness.

When we were born, we were born with the most precious gift: the gift of possibility. When you were born, you had the possibility, with the right effort, sacrifice, and focus to become anything you wanted.

But by the time we turn 18, it's as if the world has closed down on us and we end up restricted to a certain social level, a certain intellectual level, and a certain class level. In other words, we are born free, but by the time we become adults we are slaves.

No one does this to us. We do it to ourselves. We suddenly decide something is too difficult, or we lack the traits to accomplish something.

We allow ourselves to be so greatly limited that most of us end up living mediocre lives. Most of us never reach our fullest potential.

This is a matter of choice. You don't have to choose this kind of life. You can choose greatness and a life of full potential and possibility.

Your self-perception and self-image is what truly matters.

Sure, there is such a thing as objective reality. But objective reality isn't going to serve you much if you consistently bash yourself or look at yourself in the worst way possible.

However high or low you view yourself is the shape your life will take. That will become your personal reality. You are likely overlooking yourself right now. You are likely selling yourself short and neglecting your strongest points. These are what caused your lack of happiness. The moment you wake up to these is the moment you can start taking action to become a better and happier person, not just socially but across the board.

## Chapter 13. Even *They* Had Confidence...

Most people with self-confidence suffer because deep down they feel they are somehow *lacking*.

There's a deep and profound sense of inadequacy that there's something wrong or failed about them. In this chapter, I'm going to discuss some of the most famous failures in history who showcase the strength and perseverance of the human spirit.

Take some measure of reassurance from these stories.

I've selected some personal biographies of notable people in history because they show that there is always a second chance. They show that even if the world seems as if it's out to get you, as long as you believe in yourself and focus on the right things you will come out a winner. Everything that could go wrong did, and yet they dug down deep and found enough personal confidence to carry on.

If anything, all of these stories should tell you that,

regardless of how hard you have it, there were others who achieved the highest levels of success despite even greater disadvantages than yours.

Confidence is knowing that you can overcome whatever comes at you – if not the first time, the second or third time. These stories showcase this ability and should serve to inspire you to do the same. Everyone was out of their comfort zone and experienced failure, sometimes devastating.

In other words, you think you have reason to lack confidence? Read on.

## Stephen King

Stephen King is a best-selling author that is a millionaire many times over.

Many of his books have been made into movies. In fact, Stephen King's box office output is nothing short of amazing. It's easy to admire Stephen King now, but it's worth noting that his first book was actually rejected 30 times.

In fact, he was rejected so often that by the 30th rejection, he threw the book in the trash. He was on the verge of giving up writing altogether.

His first book was *Carrie*. The only reason you've heard of this seminal horror novel and movie is because Stephen King's wife saved the book by picking the pages out of the trashcan and encouraging King to follow through with his efforts at getting his book published.

At the time, this was quite a tall order that didn't have high odds of success: Stephen King was living with his wife and two kids in a trailer in Maine. He had most recently worked at a laundromat, and was starting a teaching position at a local high school.

Not only was he barely making ends meet, the teaching job left him with very little energy or time to spare at the end of the day.

Thanks to his wife, who encouraged him to keep pushing forward with his book, he kept shopping the book until a major publishing house decided to buy his novel.

In fact, Stephen King was so broke that his publisher *telegrammed* him the approval notice. Why? King had his telephone removed to save money.

Just how successful is Stephen King now? He's had four movies created from his books. He has a catalog of best-selling books. He even has a Broadway musical under his belt.

**Harlan David Sanders**

Who is this?

Why, it's Colonel Sanders from Kentucky Fried Chicken (KFC)!

Colonel Sanders started his KFC dream at the ripe old age of

65.

Let's think of it this way — at that ripe old age, most people think about retiring. They don't think about starting a business.

But this wasn't an intentional second career that he started to fill his time. The reason Colonel Sanders got a late start to the restaurant chain that would later be a global giant was because until then he'd lived a life of failure.

During the Great Depression, he decided to sell chicken at a roadside gas station. Money was so tight that he converted his personal living quarters next to the gas station into a fried chicken restaurant. Over the next decade, he perfected the secret recipe that KFC is internationally known for. Yet that same recipe was rejected over 1,009 times by commercial restaurants and chains.

Even with a small measure of success, the highway was rerouted from his restaurant over the years and, almost broke, he was forced to close his restaurant.

Because he was stuck with a monthly pension of a $105, he hit the road trying to find restaurants that would franchise or effectively rent out the rights to his secret chicken recipe. He just wanted a nickel for each piece of chicken the franchisee restaurant sold using his recipe. He would often drive around and sleep in his car to solicit restaurants to use his recipe. The first 1000 times, he failed.

As of 2013, there were 18,875 KFC outlets all over the world, located in 118 countries and territories. In China alone there were 4563 KFC outlets. That number has probably gone up since then. KFC is a multibillion dollar global company, and it would not have happened if Colonel Sanders had given up when his restaurant business was forced to shut down. It would also not have happened if he had taken those 1000 rejections personally.

Still, he persevered when he had no reason to and the world is a tastier place thanks to his efforts.

**Henry Ford**

Yes, that Ford. You might even be driving the great-great-grand-grandchild of one of his cars.

Henry Ford is the man who essentially invented the modern automobile, revolutionized the assembly line, and whose company is still one of the biggest car manufacturers in America.

Ford motor vehicles are found pretty much all over the planet, and Henry Ford is one of the most powerful pioneers in the global automotive industry.

But these achievements almost never happened.

Ford failed spectacularly several times before achieving success. In fact, he had to file bankruptcy twice before forming Ford Motor Company. An additional failure was when he was kicked out of a car company he helped found, now known as Cadillac.

This man was no stranger to failure, but what made him different and stand apart from all the other geniuses out there was that he never gave up.

He decided to keep pushing forward with his vision and now the world is much richer because of his efforts.

Genius and success are often equated with each other. A lot of people are under the misconception that to be successful in life, they only need to have the smarts and everything will work—not true. You may have all the potential in the world, but if you do not stick with it and if you give up too quickly you will not achieve the success you were destined to achieve. Everybody's destined for greatness. We all have the capacity of greatness. The problem is too many of us simply give up.

The three real-life stories that I mentioned highlight people who have tremendous potential just like everybody. What separates them from us and what makes them household names now is because they never gave up.

Focus on what your dreams are. Focus on what your ideals are. Never give up on them. Life can throw you a curve ball from time to time, but what matters is not that you get knocked down, what matters more is how quickly you get back up.

That's true confidence.

## Chapter 14. Instant Social Confidence Tactics

This chapter is action-focused and action-packed.

It's full of confidence tactics you can use within the next 24 hours to increase your social confidence and be comfortable in any situation.

These aren't just tips for your success. These are tips that will make you feel more confident and in control by making situations that normally worry you more predictable.

As we know, lack of social confidence is almost always rooted in lack of experience and perceived lack of control – *I don't know what can go wrong but I know it'll be bad!*

These tactics take care of that fear of having the safety net yanked away.

### Warm Up

We did cover this earlier in the book, but it's worth a

second mention because it's one of the most valuable social confidence tactics in existence.

Warm up by reading out loud and increasing the range of your emotional expressiveness, use external stimuli, or get primed physically.

These are all designed to get you in "the zone" when it comes to social situations, just as athletes warm up their muscles in anticipation of a big competition. Your competitions are meetings, parties, and networking events. Get ready!

## Shift Attention

Whenever you're talking to someone, whether alone or in a group, it's always a good idea to divert the focus onto other people.

You win in two ways.

First, people like to talk about themselves. People like to be the center of attention, so give them the spotlight. The more you focus on them, the less focus will be on you. You create an atmosphere of comfort and familiarity, while avoiding the spotlight if you don't quite feel ready or up to it.

The second way you win is you have more time to get acclimated and not say things you might regret saying because your mind blanked. Feel free to chime in where you can. This enables you to have plenty of time to think about what to say.

This is one of those situations where it is much better to give than receive.

It's not enough just to pass the microphone to someone else in the group. You also have to be an active listener and do your part in facilitating the conversation flow.

You can't just give up all responsibility for the social interaction and put it on the shoulders of the person you're speaking with. They have to feel engaged enough to keep telling stories and sharing personal information.

The easiest way to do this is to show intense interest and curiosity.

**Break Out of Groups**

As much as possible, try to avoid talking to multiple people at once (in a circle, for example).

Whenever you're talking to more than one person, it's often difficult to manage, and can be damaging to your social confidence in the moment when you can't capture the sole attention of the person you are speaking to.

In other words, there's always the possibility that you're sending your message into the abyss. That's fine once or twice, but imagine a situation where you make 10 statements, and 9 times people only give you a polite chuckle and return to the other people in the group.

So try to break out of groups and keep things on an

engaged, one-to-one level. Simply turn towards the person next to you and ask them with a lower volume of voice a question about them specifically so it's clear that it's not intended for the group at large.

This allows you to engage more easily. You also only have to manage one person. You'll get far more positive feedback, and it will only serve to grow your social confidence.

**Be the Host**

If you take it upon yourself to organize an event or play host, this can help you overcome your social confidence issues.

This may sound counterintuitive, but the role of a host or organizer comes with an inherent position of power. Instinctively, people will look up to you and seek you out.

They will place an expectation on you, and you will rise to meet them naturally and easily because you are indeed in control of the entire party or event. They'll look to you to guide them, tell them where to go and eat, and also expect you to make introductions.

You're in a social situation with a clear purpose, and that's fairly predictable, isn't it? That gives us confidence because even if a conversation happens to fizzle, we can move on easily because we are in dictating the situation and also making sure things go well.

This will increase your social confidence because you can see that people are relying on you. You will feel the amount of trust they have in you.

You'll be surprised how a little bit of a push and the responsibility of being the host can trigger an untapped reservoir of social energy you didn't know you had.

If not the host, you can fabricate a role or purpose for yourself during a social situation, so you're not aimlessly trying to just "socialize." It's akin to going jogging, and actively trying to run faster, instead of running in circles. When you give yourself a purpose, you can focus on that first and foremost and keep yourself occupied.

So be proactive and choose to be the host of a social event.

**Fallback Stories**

Any healthy conversation will have dead spots, this cannot be avoided.

Even if you're the best conversationalist in the world, there will always be twists and turns in any conversation that lead to dead spots.

Therefore, you should prepare for them by having a few topics ready. By quickly pivoting to these topics, you will be able to defeat an incoming awkward silence. You pre-empt the dead spots in your conversation.

It's important that you make sure these topics are relatable to both you and the person you're speaking with.

If the person could not care less about the topic you bring

up, then the awkward silence you fear will happen sooner rather than later.

This is why easy fallback stories are made of interpersonal issues and conflicts, because everyone has those. Not everyone has a clear opinion on the movie you saw, current events, or your work. But everyone has an opinion on interpersonal issues and conflicts.

For example, "A friend of mine just got proposed to by his girlfriend, what do you think of female proposals?"

Pose questions that do not involve you directly but can lead to differences of opinion. Of course, you need to manage your differences of opinion as well. You're not looking for a debate. You're looking to just push the conversation along in an interesting and lively way.

**Memorize Stories**

As much as possible, try to memorize the stories and your answers to the most predictable questions you're likely to be asked in any kind of social situation.

Memorize these stories and answers so you will never run out things to talk about.

One of the most common question you'll be asked is, "How was your weekend?" By coming up with funny, interesting, or engaging stories you kill two birds with one stone.

First, you keep the momentum of the conversation going or take it to a higher level. Second, you come off as an interesting person because when you've memorized interesting and engaging stories as responses to common questions, you stand out from the crowd.

You pick your best memory and shape the impression you want to make to others, and they can't help being intrigued and entertained by your story.

**Find Others to Assist**

Failing everything else, if you find yourself in a setting with strangers, try to look around the room for kindred spirits.

Chances are high you will find others that also suffer from a lack of social confidence. Make your way to them and introduce yourself. The strategy here is to find others you might feel socially superior to. These are people you can feel more confident around. Find people who look bored or are standing alone and wishing they had someone to talk to.

You know you've been in their shoes and that they will be very happy and grateful that you've engaged them. This is also a huge boost to your social confidence – this person is happy to see you and speak to you. It's the consummate win-win situation.

This is also a good way to warm up in social situations if you didn't take the time beforehand to prepare yourself. You can use this interaction with a low-confidence person to assume the role of the talker and the outgoing extrovert for a bit. You know they will react positively to you, which will create that positive feedback loop we are always looking for to make you feel socially invincible.

## Chapter 15. How to be Assertive

One of the fundamental aspects of massive social confidence is getting what you want from people, but not upsetting them or making them feel used.

You're also not manipulating them. You're just asserting yourself in way that everyone feels comfortable with.

But guess what? The person who is typically the most uncomfortable with being assertive is almost always you.

There was a legendary story of passive-aggressiveness when I was in college.

It started as the tale of roommates who were too polite to be assertive. Soon, they started leaving each other post-it notes all over their room asking each other to do things (or not to do things) while simultaneously being sweet as can be face-to-face.

Eventually, this escalated to where one of the roommates

exploded and beat the other one up with a huge box of post-its. And this all could have been prevented with clear, assertive communication.

It's probably not a true story; it always rang more like a fable to me, one that was trying to teach a lesson.

But the lesson is important.

We resort to all types of coping behavior when we aren't confident and assertive with others. We do this for a variety of reasons, including but not limited to wanting to accommodate others, putting the needs of others above our own, or just plain old fearing confrontation.

Or it might be that accommodating others and giving others their way is the only value that low confidence people feel they bring to the table. And they fear the moment they stop bending over backwards is the moment people will stop liking them.

Without confident assertion, you'll be creating one of two scenarios: (1) one where you get a box of post-its jammed into your eye socket or (2) one where you become a real pushover whom others take advantage of. It's just human nature to take a mile when given an inch.

And of course, how dejected does it feel not to be able to assert oneself, even your thoughts, in a social situation? This is when you want to go against the grain, peer pressure, popular opinion, and the status quo.

Developing the skill of asserting yourself is essentially

learning how to keep yourself happy and stay on your schedule and needs instead of bending to those of other people.

**What is being assertive?**

Being assertive is simply saying you know what you want and making sure your rights and desires aren't being ignored.

Many people with low social confidence think that the moment they assert themselves, they will come off as selfish assholes. They assume that being assertive makes them arrogant, ignorant, oblivious, and un-empathetic. They are scared of stepping on the toes of the people around them and making the wrong impression. You are giving up a tremendous amount of personal dignity for what?

This is plain wrong. You're the only one who thinks that way, and ironically you're the only one who has your best interests at heart, so it's a bit of a mental contradiction.

You matter too. What you bring to the table should not be devalued, overlooked or, worse, taken for granted.

Deep down, you know this to be true. Most unassertive people and people lacking social confidence feel slighted and wronged when they let their fears get the best of them.

Much of the time, their frustration leaks out in the form of passive aggressive behavior.

This occurs when you want to express yourself, but you feel that you can't directly. The resentment builds until you can't hold it in any longer and you start lashing out in a covert, guerilla manner; Post-it notes, sneakily untying someone's shoes, and generally making their day worse in an indirect and covert way.

You just can't rely on people to read your mind via your passive-aggressive behavior. Your "clear" hints are probably not all that clear, and you are the only one fixating on the problem.

So here's the crux of the problem. We aren't confidently assertive because we feel responsible for how others feel. Even if they've caused a problem, we don't want to cause the same problem when it can easily be ignored.

That's fine when it happens on occasion. But when it happens eight times in a row, you can start to question your self-worth.

*You're not responsible for how others feel.* If they feel bad, then too bad.

Most of the time, when people assert themselves, they're just claiming their rights and making things the way they feel is fair. Don't you owe yourself that?

Lack of assertiveness is rooted in being too invested and emotionally close to a situation to see it for what it is.

You need an objective sanity test to evaluate whether your assertive intuition is correct.

This has two simple steps.

The first step is to ask yourself what you would tell a friend if they told you about the circumstances that you are in. This allows you to objectively separate emotion from reality. Objectively, would they being acting sane and reasonable if they reacted the way you did?

The second step is to actively focus on only the actions that were taken, and not the emotions and small details that were involved. Because the small details are what make the difference to you when you're emotionally close to a situation, but don't matter in the grand scheme of things. These are the *Buts* and *Waits* that infect our brains.

For example, he beat me but he told me he loved me yesterday. Does that detail matter?

We may sometimes feel justified in our assertions, but that doesn't mean we can actually utter the words. This is because we always have to add something to alleviate that slight moment of confusion and discomfort.

*Can you help me move tomorrow morning?*
*No, I don't think so, my friend is coming over.*
*Well, I really need it.*
*Well… [this is where the discomfort is] okay. Let me see what I can do.*

True assertion is as simple as not adding something to alleviate that moment but rather adding something to justify your decision, then sticking to your guns through repetition if the other person continues to persist.

*[Psst... If they are the type to continue to persist, isn't it a bit concerning that they would actively get you to change your stance despite your repeated refusals?]*

So you're just asserting, stating a reason to alleviate discomfort, and repeating.

If you feel silly repeating yourself, you should keep in mind that the other person is forcing you to because they are repeating themselves.

*Can you help me move tomorrow morning?*
*No, I don't think so, my friend is coming over.*
*Well, I really need it.*
*Sorry, bad timing. My friend is coming over tomorrow in the morning.*

You shouldn't feel any guilt for essentially being forced to volunteer yourself. They asked, and you said no. You're under no duty or obligation here.

The key is not to give in; to continue repeating your reason and not acknowledge their request. They have a right to what they need, but you also have the right to ignore their request. Maybe there are other things more important going on in your life. Maybe you have more pressing priorities. Whatever your reason, stand up for yourself.

Finally, the absence of a good excuse not to help Bob move isn't a reason to help him. In other words, it's fine not to have a reason at all. Just repeat your refusal, and if they get mad that you aren't willingly volunteering yourself for pain and suffering – that's mighty presumptuous and self-absorbed of the other person, wouldn't you say?

Here's the only caveat to embodying assertiveness.

In the beginning, your friends, coworkers, and acquaintances might not know how to take it. They might treat you oddly or hold you at arm's length.

*What's wrong with you, you're so different!*

Well, they've just seen a new side of you that they're not used to. They might not like it because until now the entire relationship dynamic was one-sided, enabling, or toxic – *in their favor*. Of course they're not wild about the change.

If they truly like you and they truly want to understand you, they will get used to it. Otherwise, they'll leave but it won't be such a great loss. They weren't your real friends in the first place – they enjoyed getting their way around you.

If you stand up for your rights and become more assertive, your real friends will get used to it and appreciate you more for it.

Here's one of the simplest exercises for social assertiveness that you can easily build upon.

When are you with one friend, initiate a selfie picture in front of something that is decidedly non-remarkable such as a statue, a street sign, or a McDonald's.

*Hey, let's take a picture here! Why? Uh... I don't know. I guess we don't have to.*

You're going to stutter, backtrack, and try to justify your decision. But you don't need to. Just as with being assertive, all you need to do is get past the barrier of that slight moment of discomfort and self-doubt.

*Hey, let's take a picture here! Why? I don't know, it's funny, let's just do it!*

Leave no room for hesitation.

Practice being assertive and telling people what you want from them. When you do this, you will get better at it because you will be able to do it with confidence. When you become comfortable with this, try doing it with more people.

Another occasion for practice involves ordering food from restaurants.

You can start by ordering for your friends or for the table. Make sure you get exactly what everyone wanted, and take charge there.

If your friends receive the wrong food, take it upon yourself to speak up immediately. Ask everyone if they want water, more napkins, and ask the staff for the bill when the time comes. This is all to practice assertiveness and get over the discomfort you feel at making requests of people.

The best part is you're operating within a safe space

because it's generally agreed that you do have a right in that particular situation to speak up. You have nothing to lose.

# Chapter 16. A 30-day Plan to Social Confidence

Coming up with an attack plan to increase your social confidence is of utmost importance because it will force you to put all that you've learned into use.

Practice and application are integral parts of learning any new skill. When you see success, you gain both confidence and you become comfortable pushing the envelope to where you want to be.

If you're trying to get better at basketball, there's only so much that reading about it will do.

Only about half of what you read will truly make sense until you actually pick up the basketball and try it for yourself. Then you can re-group and try to make better sense of what you've read.

Needless to say, this is doubly important for learning the skill of social confidence.

A theory is not going to do you much good – only consistent practice and application will change your social life for the better.

By sticking to a 30-day plan and not deviating from it, you will be forced to put the new skills into use and gradually get better at everything you do for increased social confidence.

What's special about this plan is that it uses the framework that psychiatrists use with CBT and progressive exposure therapy.

It creates a domino effect. When you deal with smaller tasks, bigger challenges start to show cracks. Take baby steps and then scale in terms of frequency and intensity. You will eventually reach a point, given enough consistent effort, for major fears to disappear.

With each small step, you will still be moving forward, no matter how insignificant it feels. This is why the plan is 30 days and not one week – it takes time, and by the end of the 30 days, you will notice a significant difference.

The moment you picked up this book, you made a deal with yourself (and me!) to commit to this plan and implement it.

### Days 1 to 4

Sit down with yourself and acknowledge that you lack social confidence. Say it to yourself and don't make excuses or rationalize why you acted in certain ways in certain situations. It's not because so-and-so was there, and it's not because you were tired that day. If that were the case, you'd be "tired" every day.

The first step is recognizing the perceived shortcoming, otherwise you will always ignore it as something you can turn on, but choose not to.

It's okay to feel a certain way.

Next, conduct a self-assessment to determine what kinds of specific situations you feel you lack social confidence in. Are there common themes as to what drains you and makes you feel unsure of yourself? Is it when there is no clear objective, or when you have expectations and watching eyes? Are there certain contexts that make you panic, or is it just a generalized discomfort?

Now start noticing some of the negative self-talk patterns that you use. Are you too hard on yourself and do you equate small setbacks to huge personality flaws? What might a bystander say about your self-evaluations?

Identify as many as possible, write them down, and then start rephrasing them in more positive and realistic terms. If you think about the consequences, write down what you think the realistic consequences will be in the next 24 hours. Because chances are, there aren't any beyond that.

Finally, read up on true social anxiety, the real mental illnesses, and consider if you need professional help.

There are certain situations where your physical symptoms are so unbearable and so pronounced that you have no other option but to get professional help. There's a huge difference between discomfort and a lack of social confidence and true mental illness.

The good news is that there is a wide range of therapy options available to you—starting with talk therapy all the way to pharmaceutical intervention.

True social anxiety can be remedied and treatment has enabled people to truly and consistently manage their clinically diagnosed social anxiety issues.

## Days 5 to 9

It's time to start thinking about what happens on a daily basis.

Think about the external stimuli and other triggers that make you feel good and confident. Be as clear as possible about them. Is it a location, a thought, remembering your past accomplishments, singing along to a loud song, or jumping up and down?

What gets in you in the zone?

This is also where you should start evaluating the skills that make you feel good and what you can cultivate.

What existing strengths can you build on? Which of your social skills can you hang your hat on? What experiences do you have that are unique and noteworthy?

The good news about all this is that regardless of how low

your social confidence level may be there is always at least one element to your personality or one set of things that produces positive social feedback. Focus on that.

You don't need a breakthrough skillset. Just anything positive and you should have more than enough to work with.

**Days 10 to 15**

This is the last portion of the program where you are working on yourself and your internal mindset before approaching other people.

This is the last set of days where you are internally steeling yourself; the rest involves actual practice and social situations. I want you to feel as prepared as possible when the time comes.

Even so, each portion is of equal value. If you neglect earlier portions, you're jumping straight into the deep end with no life preserver. You just may drown and forever be scarred by your bad experience. So give equal importance to all 30 days of this program!

For Days 10 to 15, you will create answers to the questions you know you'll be asked in small talk.

The first step to this, of course, is to list all the common questions people normally ask in social interactions. These are fairly shallow, predictable, and generic questions. You shouldn't have any difficulty coming up with this list.

Once you have your list of questions, your next step is to come up with answers to them.

The reason you're doing this is twofold. First, when people ask you questions, you will have a prepared, engaging answer that will make you appear interesting and confident. Second, this makes your conversations more predictable as a whole and that will make you feel more comfortable and confident.

During this period, you also need to question your physical appearance and presentation so you can venture into the world without doubts.

Look at yourself in the mirror when you imagine yourself talking in a small circle of strangers. What small things can you improve in easy ways?

Focus on small things like your posture, the way you move your hands, or the way you position your arms. Look at your haircut and clothes. Is there a wardrobe set or a haircut that would make you look more confident? Are there changes to your appearance that would highlight the internal confidence you already have about certain skillsets and experiences?

You might not like the new look because it feels like a costume or "not you," but perhaps "you" wasn't working that well anyway and you need to step out of your tiny comfort zone.

Continue to tweak your appearance until you're not only happy on a cosmetic level with the way you look, but you also project a higher degree of confidence.

Finally, in this stage, you should take one of your main insecurities and start creating an action plan to improve upon it. Not only will you be getting additional confidence through making social situations more predictable, you are eliminating further sources of insecurity.

**Days 16 to 20**

It's time to start looking externally and building social confidence through exposure.

By this stage, you have already prepared your mindset and your approach. You have consistently gone over the previous steps and you're ready to start taking action. The first thing you need to do is incrementally expose yourself to various social situations and tallying up your small victories.

First, you need to define what constitutes a victory for you. For some, it will be holding extended eye contact, or starting a conversation with a complete stranger. For others, it will be ordering food or coffee confidently or making a joke in front of others. Other possibilities include asking someone for what you want or touching someone on the arm, holding the door open for someone, or confidently saying "please" and "thank you" to others.

Each day, get four small victories. That's all it takes.

On Days 19 and 20, shoot for bigger victories.

Chances are that there will have been zero negative repercussions in the first three days. Remember that. What's to fear? Shoot higher.

**Days 21 to 25**

Continue getting at least four victories a day, though by this point they should have increased a bit in size and grandeur.

Start noticing (1) your bad habits in conversations, and (2) conversational patterns after you have gotten your feet wet with some good interactions and small victories.

The good news is you should be able to do this during your small victories, which should feel easier and easier.

Take note of what reactions you can get with different phrases. Take note of areas where you can improve. Take note of what stories and jokes never get any chuckles.

Refer constantly to the index card you created based on an earlier chapter of this book. Make sure that noticing your bad habits doesn't undo how you feel about your strengths.

The point here is that you are going to be building on your strengths and spotlighting your bad habits so you can work toward eliminating them.

**Days 26 to 30**

Implement the confidence tactics and assertiveness tips that you read earlier in this book.

This is the stage where you are more desensitized to daily social situations, and can think clearly about how you are representing yourself in them as opposed to making sure that you don't just melt into a pile of stuttering.

Your quota is to add five medium-sized victories a day. If you keep this up, you will eventually reach a point of momentum.

The point of momentum to look out for is when it's so much harder to stop than to start. You know that you're on a roll. You know that you are already getting used to interacting a certain way. It's only a matter of time until your biggest fears start melting away.

## Chapter 17. Introvert Confidence

Introversion is one of the elephants in the room that I wanted to address last.

What if you think you're an introvert, and that's the source of your lack of social confidence?

Well, there are a lot of misconceptions about what it means to be an introvert.

People assume that introverts are shy and socially awkward, and because of that, there is something fundamentally wrong with them. That they don't like social situations, and border on anti-social and loner tendencies.

These are unfortunate definitions and associations.

Introverts are not necessarily shy, as people think – they simply have a limited amount of social energy that they can devote to social relationships and activities. Extroverts, on the other hand, actually get their energy from being around others.

While an extrovert's batteries are recharged when he or she is socially engaged, an introvert's batteries are quickly depleted. Introverts recharge by being alone. So on the surface, an introvert may appear shy – but that isn't because that's their natural disposition. They're just tired, and their social batteries are exhausted for the time being.

Here's what it feels like for introverts: suppose you had just run a marathon. An introvert might think, "That's enough fitness for now!" An extrovert would say the equivalent of *"Let's run another five miles!"*

An introvert may seem awkward, socially unconfident and uncomfortable, but that's an illusion. A truly socially unconfident person might be that way because others make him uncomfortable.
But the introvert only appears to lack social confidence on the outside – they enjoy socializing and can be very good at it – it's just that they can't and don't want to do it for too long. So when an introvert seems unconfident, you're just catching them at the end of their battery.

Externally, there may not seem to be much of a difference between a shy and socially awkward person and an introvert, but you have to look past appearances to understand how they are different.

**Introvert Tendencies**

Introverts tend to burn up a lot of energy just being around other people. This energy drain can interfere with their need for introspection and thinking time. Just because being social is an energy drain for an introvert does not mean they are socially incompetent or averse to spending time with others.

They just have a different operating system than extroverts. Instead of being charged up by social activity, they are worn down and need time alone to recharge.

You have to give them the opportunity to recharge their emotional batteries so that they can mingle with other people. If you frustrate this withdrawal process, it can lead to a lot of miscommunication and misunderstanding. It can lead to the introvert being completely misunderstood as anti-social or as simply not liking people.

It's not personal or about you.

**Expectations**

The key to being successful as an introvert is to know your limits.

Expect that you will hit a wall when it comes to social events.

Expect that your calendar can feel a bit overwhelming at times.

Expect to hit your limit from time to time, and learn to work around it.

If you are in a relationship with - or good friends with - an introvert, you also have to change your expectations regarding your introverted friend. You have to be understanding of their need to withdraw from time to time so that they can regain the energy level they need to be highly effective socially.

Expect that they may retreat from you without any apparent reason.

Expect that they may appear outwardly unconfident and unwilling to engage.

This doesn't mean they dislike people or that they think they are better than anyone else. It is simply because they need time to themselves – it's how they are wired.

If you are an introvert and social settings intimidate and tire you, there is no need to fear.

It is important to recognize the topics and environments that you thrive in. While focusing on certain topics that fit your passions may be a good strategy, you can do much better by picking the environments that you are going to socialize in.

When you are in the right environment, you feel eminently comfortable and in your element, and you can pick the right topics to truly blossom. Otherwise, you may feel as if you are in a threatening environment, and this can impact your social performance. Correspondingly, this can impact the quality and length of your conversations.

Here are some tips on how you can select your battlefield, so to speak, so you can win your war against social awkwardness and bad conversations.

**Focus on Predictability**

Typical introverts stay away from random bar nights. These are nights when extroverts get together with their friends, and they jump from nightclub to nightclub, bar to bar. The problem with socializing this way is that you end up mixing with people you don't know.

You end up in unfamiliar territory. This is dangerous for your social battery, as unfamiliar situations require untold amounts of social effort and attention.

The same applies for parties. If you go from place to place, you meet different people with different agendas, different purposes, and it can get quite scary. And this also applies when going to different networking groups and events.

When you go to these places, you don't know who will be there. You don't know what the agenda will be. Even though there is a central agenda, which is to develop business, this can lead to all sorts of awkward and intimidating social contacts.

Focus on the places and social settings you know you will be comfortable in and that you know there will be few surprises in. By chasing after predictability, you can increase the likelihood that your social interactions will be successful, and you can even have more of them. You can increase the probability that you will display the classic traits of an extrovert.

**Focus on Your Interests**

Do this quick exercise.

Sit down and list the places and situations where you feel most comfortable. You might be comfortable hanging out at a cafe. Hanging out at a park, or taking long walks might set you at ease. Bike trips, hiking or camping with a few close friends might be your thing.

Regardless of the particular situation or the particular place, write it down. What is important here is that you have a pure list of the things, activities, or places where you are most comfortable.

Now that you have a clear idea of the context that you are very comfortable in, the next step is to engage in those activities and put yourself in those places. Chances are high that the conversations you will get into will be longer, more engaging, and positive because you are at ease. Know your comfort level. This allows your social battery to run off its reserves because it doesn't have to deal with anything new and can focus on the task at hand.

Know where your areas of strength are and focus on those.

**Develop Exit Strategies**

You can't always control the place you find yourself in.

This is why you need an exit strategy. Know how to withdraw. Know how to get out of the situation and how to do it *smoothly*.

Introverts who are socially awkward tend to exit in the roughest way possible leaving behind a bad impression. As a result, other people will get the wrong picture. You want to free yourself from that unnecessary drama and misunderstanding.

You want to avoid those social problems by having a smooth exit strategy for unpleasant social situations. Isn't it high time that you have a strategy that allows you to withdraw from unpleasant or uncomfortable social situations – without looking like a fool, rude, or socially awkward?

Here are a few quick suggestions.

First, have an excuse ready to leave any conversation or social situation. The bathroom, needing to call someone, or searching for someone else always works.

Second, act as if the need for an exit is urgent, so the other people in your context won't take it personally or question it.

Finally, apologize for having to leave! Be regretful. Drive home the genuineness of your need to go and let people know that you are remorseful about the fact that you need to exit.

These three steps can help you build an exit strategy for wherever you go, and whatever situation you find yourself in.

**Focus on Silent Activities**

Social batteries measure different things for different people, but most commonly they measure how much you want to interact with another human being.

If this is indeed what your social battery measures, then you are in luck. You should still consider yourself able to spend time with others and engage in social situations, but you just have to limit them to silent activities.

Working on a puzzle with friends, running with a friend, or any other activity where talking and interaction is secondary to the activity itself.

So actually, this point is contrary to the title of the chapter stating that you need to select specific social environments that preserve your social battery. You actually have a bit more leeway in the social environments that you find yourself in if you can also engage in silent activities with other people.

To others and to the casual observer, it will appear that you are still being as social as anyone else, but little do they know that you've taken advantage of a silent group activity for your own benefit!

## Conclusion

As you might have surmised, at some point, I was able to successfully reverse the years of programming from my negative self-talk about public speaking.

It wasn't without ups and downs, but I ended up founding a fairly prominent a capella singing group during my college years.

Once you're on stage in front of thousands of people singing, spitting, and dancing, public speaking doesn't have quite the same anxious effect anymore.

It was my own version of accelerated exposure therapy.

Social confidence is not simply the ability to talk to people you want. It's the ability to live freely and see a world of possibility, instead of attack and judgment.

Suppose that you have the choice of which path to take? It's an easy decision, isn't it?

Sincerely,

Patrick King
Social Interaction Specialist
www.PatrickKingConsulting.com

P.S. If you enjoyed this book, please don't be shy and drop me a line, leave a review, or both! I love reading feedback, and reviews are the lifeblood of Kindle books, so they are always welcome and greatly appreciated.

**Other books by Patrick King include:**

**Conversation Tactics: Strategies to Command Social Situations: Wittiness, Banter, Likability**

## Speaking and Coaching

Imagine going far beyond the contents of this book and dramatically improving the way you interact with the world and the relationships you'll build.

Are you interested in contacting Patrick for:

- A social skills workshop for your workplace
- Speaking engagements on the power of conversation and charisma
- Personalized social skills and conversation coaching

Patrick speaks around the world to help people improve their lives through the power of building relationships with improved social skills. He is a recognized industry expert, bestselling author, and speaker.

To invite Patrick to speak at your next event or to inquire about coaching, get in touch directly through his website's contact form at http://www.PatrickKingConsulting.com/contact, or contact him directly at Patrick@patrickkingconsulting.com.

**Cheat Sheet**

## Chapter 1. The Ripple Effect of Social Confidence

Possessing social confidence or not has a startling ripple effect on how you live your life and the innate expectations you carry with you.

## Chapter 2. Banish Your Negative Self-Talk

Negative self-talk is often overly influenced by emotion and actively disempowers you with a story you create about yourself. That story that began as a perception becomes your reality.

## Chapter 3. Your Social Confidence Self-Assessment

To make any kind of meaningful headway, it's imperative to have a baseline from which to begin and improve. Do you feel more comfortable in situations where you have boundaries, or do you prefer zero expectations and freedom?

## Chapter 4. Apples to Bananas Comparisons

Comparisons are one of the worst detriments to social confidence because you use your worst moments with someone else's filtered, best moments. It's a game you can never win.

## Chapter 5. Incremental Skill Cultivation

The bedrock of confidence is often skills. All of us feel capable and confident in something, so it's about finding that aspect of social interactions that we can hang out hat on and branching out from it.

## Chapter 6. How to be "In The Zone" for Any Social Situation

Various ways of warming yourself up for social situations include reading out loud, visualizing to prepare, carrying around your confidence resume, and various external stimuli.

## Chapter 7. Taking Action Against Insecurity

Taking action against the low-hanging fruit of insecurity might just be enough to grow your confidence levels.

## Chapter 8. Is it Clinical?

Social anxiety is a real, clinical problem that is highly differentiated from a lack of social confidence. Symptoms are severe and crippling, and fear essentially dictates life choices.

## Chapter 9. Slaying the Dragon

Incremental exposure therapy has long been the preferred method of overcoming fears and anxieties. For example, dealing with your fear in a lesser or controlled manner, to become accustomed to the feeling of tension.

## Chapter 10. The Art of Self-Acceptance

Self-acceptance is about realizing the myth of perfection, and realizing the strengths that you truly have.

## Chapter 11. Toxic, Draining Habits

Chances are you are engaging in toxic habits that continually beat down your self-worth and highlight your weaknesses, consciously or subconsciously.

## Chapter 12. Social Confidence Perspectives

This chapter is a collection of perspectives and quotes on confidence, and the common threads are that we live in self-imposed prison cells that are both powerful yet non-existent.

## Chapter 13. Even They Had Confidence...

Three famous, household figures suffered more setbacks than you ever had in your life. Yet their names still found their way to your lips.

## Chapter 14. Instant Social Confidence Tactics

More than confidence, there are various tactics to use in social situations to make sure that you feel comfortable throughout, such as memorizing stories, shifting the attention to others, and placing yourself in a position of inherent power.

## Chapter 15. How to be Assertive

Being assertive is the power to overcome the split-second of tension when you face confrontation. If you face the possibility of upsetting someone, you're not responsible for how others feel.

## Chapter 16. A 30-day Plan to Social Confidence

The 30-day plan consists of two distinct portions – creating internal mindsets and in-field practice and exposure.

## Chapter 17. Introvert Confidence

There are various tactics you can use to settle expectations when dealing with introverts, and to save and recharge their relatively fickle social batteries.

Made in the USA
Middletown, DE
16 February 2017